FREDERICA:

I enjoyed our conversation for the radio interview. I hope you find this book interesting, entertaining and perhaps a bit enlightening . . .

6/17

SHIFT THE NARRATIVE

Russell Rendenbaugh

FREDERICA:

I enjoyed our conversation for the radio interview. I hope you find this book interesting, entertaining and perhaps a bit enlightening . . .

SHIFT THE NARRATIVE

A BLIND MAN'S VISION FOR REWRITING THE STORIES THAT LIMIT US

RUSSELL REDENBAUGH

NEW YORK

NASHVILLE • MELBOURNE • VANCOUVER

SHIFT THE NARRATIVE
A BLIND MAN'S VISION FOR REWRITING
THE STORIES THAT LIMIT US

© 2017 **RUSSELL REDENBAUGH**

Published in New York, New York, by Morgan James Publishing. Morgan James is a trademark of Morgan James, LLC. www.MorganJamesPublishing.com

The Morgan James Speakers Group can bring authors to your live event. For more information or to book an event visit The Morgan James Speakers Group at www.TheMorganJamesSpeakersGroup.com.

ISBN 978-1-63047-498-0 paperback
ISBN 978-1-63047-738-7 eBook
ISBN 978-1-68350-219-7 hardcover
Library of Congress Control Number: 2016914544

Interior Design by:
Bonnie Bushman
The Whole Caboodle Graphic Design

DEDICATION

To my wife Natalia, who is the light of my life,
revealing what I don't see.

CONTENTS

ACKNOWLEDGMENTS

I offer my sincerest thanks:

To my cousin and friend, Brent Bingham, who taught me how to rock climb.

To my clients, past and future, for their trust in my ability to "read the world."

To Dean Blanchard of Wharton who gave me a chance to prove I could do the work and be employable, and to the Wharton school for making an investment in me that paid off for us both.

To my brother, David, my first best friend who I miss to this day.

To the many family and friends who did not let me give up on myself.

To Dr. Fernando Flores who, quite frankly, taught me how to think.

To my Uncle Jake Garn, United States Senator and space shuttle astronaut, who visited me in the hospital for forty-two days straight.

To George Gilder who taught me to listen to technology and how it changes the economy by changing the relative prices of factors of production.

To all the neighbors that day in Salt Lake City who rushed to my aid, especially Ruth Johnson, the nurse who saved my life.

To James Juliano, my business partner and friend, who despite being my protege, has taught me much about investing and life.

To Dr. Art Laffer, who taught me serious economics.

To Dr. Drew Lebby, my dear friend and trusted advisor for over thirty-five years.

To James Christopher Adams McClennen who gave me the chance to prove I could learn to invest.

To my fraternity brother, Kendall Oldroyd, who encouraged me during what appeared to be a futile job search during graduate school with his words, "if you were a stock I would invest in you."

To pro-growth policymakers and economists who carry the torch of prosperity.

To Stanford and Harvard for rejecting my graduate school applications. They join the large list who said, "You can't."

To Christine Whitmarsh for her professionalism and knowledge of the book space. I would never advise a friend to start a book without Christine as the project's producer. She helped turn my idea of writing a book into the reality of a completed one.

FOREWORD

Is your life in need of a shift? Do you feel that you are drifting through your existence, pushed down by forces beyond your control, mired in a meager narrative by the pressure of circumstance, your ceiling capped, your future a dreary repetition of the past?

Do you believe you have free will to change course? Do you believe that your life can be transformed, not merely by small increments but by radical new shifts of direction and resolve?

Many of you think you are beyond such concerns. Many of you already deem yourselves successful. Complacent about your career and accomplishments, you want to cruise forward without rocking any boats or risking any setbacks on the road to a comfortable retirement. But everyone, from our new President Trump to a homeless man on the streets, from an investor who diversifies his holdings into mediocrity, to a business executive who hesitates to act in the face of apparent risks, from an unmarried mother mired in the welfare state to a Senator paralyzed by polls and press and precedent, needs to grasp the crucial truths about change and redemption luminously expounded in this book.

"What story is trapping you?" Redenbaugh asks. "What story will free you to move forward? That is the story you need. That is your new narrative."

Most of us are never required to break from the drab drift of mediocrity. Most of us, says Redenbaugh in this guidebook for human achievement, never discover the real dimensions of human possibility. We are creatures of habit and happenstance, drift and drudgery. We are believers in the imperial privileges of what already exists, rather than authors of the narrative of our lives of change.

Many historians, economists and other experts imagine that America has reached this kind of impasse. We have come to the end of the American frontier and fathomed the limits of the world. With a huge overhang of debt, massive encrustation of laws and rules, looming challenges of aging and disability, "climate change" and overpopulation, our horizons seem to be closing in on us. Compared to previous eras of industrial revolution and creativity, leading government and university economists see an era of "secular stagnation" at hand, an era of dismal stasis and decline, as technology loses its creative dynamism and enterprise faces a disabled destiny.

Dominant in government and the universities, a "cautionary principle"—safety first and foremost—has unleashed regulatory webs of rules that stifle enterprise, invention, and energy production. Climate change allegedly portends a steady shrinkage in the world's population, prosperity, and resources. Diminishing energy supplies doom entrepreneurial initiative and manufacturing expansion. We face a future of darkness on a disabled planet.

In this predicament, we search for a seer to guide us. We desire a visionary who can see through the shadows to find the light beyond. We need an explorer who is not bound by the existing maps and narratives of our possibilities. We need a man who can navigate the tenebrous turmoil of our times.

We need an explorer of human accomplishment who can tell us how to transcend a future that seems both dark and disabled. Providentially today, in this extraordinary manual of human triumph, we have the vision and wisdom that springs from the unique experiences of Redenbaugh. "Most people," he writes, "do not think about their lives until it is too late. Then they think only about their regrets." Despite his harrowing privations, Redenbaugh has lived a life of no regrets. This book gives us a lucid agenda for a radical shift in our own lives and in the future of our nation that will banish all regrets that stem from living too little and too lamely.

To Russell, the current human predicament is just life as he has known it from the age of 17. At that point, inspired by President Kennedy's declaration that by the end of the decade America would put a man on the moon and bring him back alive, the young Redenbaugh attempted to build and launch a solid state rocket out of an aluminum tube and some handmade gunpowder. The resulting explosion mangled his hands and caused him to lose his eyesight, first in one eye and then the other despite a prolonged purgatory of some 30 surgeries. He was plunged into a life of darkness and disability. He was told he was destined to a regime of "welfare, unemployment, and dependency." His mother decided that he could never marry, attend a prestigious university, or even leave home.

It was the cautionary principle in practice. The world told Russell that he could not risk college, enterprise, marriage or aspiration. He was condemned to the darkness of impotence and dependency.

This is our situation today as a nation. We incur debt to sustain 10 millions of able young men without work and out of the workforce. We enact minimum wage laws that suppress the very starting jobs they need. We wrap the disabled in layers of programs and supports that end up making their disability insuperable.

Redenbaugh shows the path to redemption and prosperity not only intellectually but even physically and aspirationally. He became a national leader on the Civil Rights Commission, entrepreneurial creator in Silicon Valley, partner in a major investment firm, husband and father, and even a world champion fully-abled athlete after age 50. I'll leave that amazing triumph of age and guile over youth and strength for the book. It is an inspirational story for our particular times, dismissing the darkness of a spurious psychology of human limits and asserting an agenda of supreme accomplishment.

Forced to shift, defy drift, compelled to pioneer in a suddenly darkened realm beyond most of our imaginations, he became an explorer of a mostly unknown realm of human experience. He discovered that the chief obstacles to his success—and the success of other disabled people—come from the impulse to protect them from the world and the truth. In this book, he reveals his discoveries to the world, delivering a step-by-step agenda for shifts of thought, narrative, declaration, action, and perseverance that can radically change the lives of his readers and his country.

"Diversification is what you do when you don't know what to do," he writes. It means succumbing to the inexorably distracting diversity of the environment, rather than moving forward in a coherent narrative toward your own goals. In response to the upholders of the existing rulebooks that prevail over our stagnant economy, our torpid lives, he quotes Cormac McCarthy: "If the rule you followed brought you to this, what use was the rule?"

We live in an economy of mind, and an economy of mind can change as quickly as minds can change. Redenbaugh changed his mind and all else followed, as the apparent obstacles in his path gave way to opportunities, and the opportunities opened the way to yet new horizons. Key is knowing what you seek and saying it loud and publically. "When the odds are against you," he writes, "and obstacles being thrown from many directions, having strong clear declarations is what makes giving up on your narrative shift, impossible. It closes the loopholes that allow you to slip slide away from the design of your life."

Crucial is willingness to flout drift, and to shift the narrative of your life. Russell did it and so can you. God punishes you chiefly for what you fail to imagine.

There is no easy way to change the world. As Redenbaugh reports, "My friend and student Leslie learned this while attending one of my investment seminars…She said that I taught her how to 'see' and found the irony of learning to see from a blind person absolutely delicious."

I learned much from this book and predict that many people will find the experience of learning to see anew from Redenbaugh's crisp prose and compelling stories similarly delectable.

—**George Gilder**, Tyringham, Massachusetts

INTRODUCTION

February 1963

The woman sitting in a chair at the patient's bedside burst into uncontrollable tears. She was inconsolable.

The doctors had just delivered the verdict about her seventeen-year-old son, "We have done all we can do. He will be blind for the rest of his life."

The patient himself was overcome with a sense of great relief.

That patient was me. After six months of effort and five failed surgeries, the news that I was now permanently blind was a release from the uncertainty, the unknown, and the enforced idleness. My life was now open to the journey it would become...

SHIFT

This book not only steps you through some of that journey, but more importantly, highlights the model and tools that I developed as a result to help you shift the entire narrative of your life.

As was foreshadowed in the opening scene, the narrative of my own life was derailed in one irreversible moment when I was just sixteen-years-old and traumatically injured, maimed and ultimately blinded in a homemade rocket experiment gone horribly wrong. From there I had a choice to make—would I permit this new version of myself to define my life narrative moving forward? The answer was a firm no. Being blind would either limit or open my possibilities and I chose the latter. After the accident I shifted my narrative away from being a victim and declared that being blind did not mean I would be poor, dependent and homebound. I declared that I would not succumb to the narrative of what it is to be blind. I would live in the sighted world, doing things sighted people do. I lost my sight, but not my vision. In fact, losing my sight compelled me to gain vision for my future.

So I went forward, a blind person in a sighted world, with sighted goals and a vision for my life not based on physical limitations. Determined to rise above welfare, I studied finance and investment, relentless in my pursuit of success to the point of refusing to accept "no" as an answer from the admissions departments of America's top universities. The vision I had for my life was clearly much larger than the one they saw for me. The next chapters included me as a partner in a billion dollar investment firm, one of eight Commissioners on the U.S. Civil Rights Commission in Washington D.C. and helming a software company in the always exciting times of Silicon Valley. Even once I settled into my own registered investment advisory firm to act as Chief Investment Officer for wealthy families and institutions, the lens of my life vision did not narrow. Instead, at age fifty, I took up the martial art of Brazilian jiu-jitsu and with an uncompromising commitment to training, I ended up becoming the sole blind black belt in the sport and won three consecutive Brazilian jiu-jitsu World Championships fighting sighted opponents. Even with all these accomplishments though, I sometimes find myself thinking that I could have so much more.

It's unfortunate how many of us don't see all the possibilities for our lives. As an economist, I can say this is because people simply don't see the costs they're incurring by not taking the actions needed to change their lives. They are blind to the cost of not shifting their narrative. Now I'm sure that a psychologist, life coach, or other observer would give a very different answer—but I'm an economist and this is how I see and understand the world; in losses and gains, scarcity and abundance. In short, I see in terms of incentives. This view of the world, the one that will be revealed in this book, is also the reason for its title, *Shift*. Staying with economics, a shift in the supply or demand curves is not the same at all as mere movement along the curve. A shift is a drastic change in the entire height of the curve. Therefore, rest assured when I talk about "shifting your narrative," I'm not talking about temporarily "changing your life." Traditional "life changes" are fueled by motivation and inspiration, whether in book or speech form. Unfortunately, most of those messages last only until you close the book or return to your car after hearing the speech. This type of "change" is fleeting, if it even comes to fruition at all. It is often a mere decal glued over a set of ineffective habits and practices. This temporary changing of your life seems like a never-ending process of habit and ritual chores, forcing out negative thoughts, trying to replace them with positive ones. In sharp contrast, shifting your narrative is changing the "story" that may have supported you in the past but is now holding you back.

While becoming blind was an accident, my journey from welfare to wealth was not. It was an intentional narrative shift, as were the other smaller navigations along the way. I'm about to share with you how I did it. You will not merely learn how I did what I have done, but far more importantly, you will see that you can do much more with your life than you ever thought possible. This book is about the journey *your* life can become by learning to see the world as I, blind since the age of seventeen, have learned to see it.

FLYING BLIND

The Myth of the Super Survivor

There is a literature of people who started out as mere mortals and then, after surviving some enormous adversity, turned that adversity into a benefit and became very accomplished in one way or another. Whether any of this is true or not, it's still a very effective way to think about your life. Because most people don't think about their life until it's too late. Then, they think only about their regrets.

—Russell Redenbaugh

CHAPTER 1
PURGATORY

May 19, 1962

It must have been friction… or even just a spark. Something ignited the fuel, and rather than just burning, it exploded.

During the early 1960s, Americans of all ages and from all walks of life were very concerned about Communism, the Cold War, and what would subsequently be called "The Evil Empire." The (then) Soviet Union was militarily ahead of us particularly in terms of weapons and their space program. They were first in space with the first satellite and first again with a human in orbit. This wasn't OK with most of us, especially as the Space Race and Cold War were closely tied together. This was not a friendly competition to the moon to search for moon people. This was a matter of national security.

President Kennedy's declaration that, "We will put a man on the moon and bring him back alive in this decade," lit a fire under the country. There was a lot of nationalism mixed with concern that our enemies were, quite literally, taking over the world. That concern spread even to kids in high school, including myself. I was inspired by the president's challenge and became enthusiastic about all things that flew.

One Saturday morning in my hometown of Salt Lake City, eagerly anticipating summer break from the school I hated, I didn't have any work to do so I decided to feed my passion for flight. It was a warm spring day and I was working shirtless in our small garage. Outside in the sunlight, other kids played ball in the street, women worked in their gardens, and men tinkered with Chevys and Fords in their driveways. In 1962, weekends weren't designed for anything more serious.

I was making a solid-state rocket. An aluminum tube served as the body. A homemade version of gunpowder made of potassium nitrate, sulfur, and charcoal designed to slow burn rather than explode, served as the fuel. I'd obtained the sulfur from the local pharmacy and, of course, regular grade barbeque charcoal was easy to come by. Getting my hands on potassium nitrate, however, was a trickier affair. Using my motorcycle and posing as a delivery boy for Federated Milk Producers (a milk marketing co-op), I showed up at the Braun Connect Hymen chemical supply company, to pick up our one-pound order. They bought my story, and I got the third ingredient for my homemade gunpowder.

My fingertips were growing black with gunpowder and beads of sweat formed on the back of my neck in the warm, confined space as I tested different mixtures for the fuel, increasing the sulfur and charcoal incrementally to slow down the burn rate. Sitting on a bench in a small work area cordoned off in the garage, I used a dirty rag to blot at the sweat and got ready to clamp the rocket in a vise. A silver flash of light through the window temporarily blinded me as some neighborhood kids bicycled by, laughing and squealing, the bright spring sun reflecting off their bikes. I blinked hard to clear away the white spots and then returned to the task at hand, concentrating hard. After the rocket was clamped, the plan was to then ignite it with an electric spark from the magneto on my motorcycle. But I never got that far. On my way to clamp the rocket, mixing the chemicals together, something went wrong.

It must have been friction… or even just a spark. Something ignited the fuel and rather than just burning, it exploded.

The thunderous explosion could be heard several blocks away. On an otherwise lazy weekend morning, men, women, and children stopped what they were doing. They froze in place, with some even peering up anxiously at the sky believing an enemy attack was never too far off.

Back in the middle of the charred, splintered garage, a teenage boy stood stunned in place with chest, arms and face badly burned, and gushing blood from shrapnel wounds.

I was surrounded by blackness, but there was no pain—yet.

I realized the rocket had exploded. I knew I was seriously injured. I felt the warm wetness of blood flowing over my skin, on my arms, my head, my chest, and my legs. Unable to see, I ran my hand down my leg and felt a heavy puddle of blood soaking through my jeans near my thigh, near a major artery I knew of from science class. If nobody came to my rescue soon I would most likely pass out and possibly die. The time that passed was actually in my mind as it took only seconds for the entire neighborhood, mostly housewives, to descend upon the damaged garage.

Our next-door neighbor, Ruth Johnson, was an Army surgical nurse. Luckily for me it was 1962 and Ruth was gathering in her laundry that had been hanging out to dry "the old-fashioned way." She rushed into the garage where her laundered sheets and towels became my bandages and tourniquets. I was floating in and out of consciousness, bleeding heavily, burned all over, and still unable to see.

I spent forty-two days in the hospital and along with my parents, my Uncle Jake Garn (Navy pilot, U.S. Senator, and eventual Space Shuttle payload specialist) visited every single day. He came every morning on his way to work, to relieve whichever parent had spent the night on a cot in the corner of the hospital room. This daily ritual soon became automatic for him. Later on, for days after I left the hospital, Jake turned onto the street leading to the hospital every morning out of habit before realizing what he was doing and turning around.

Meanwhile in the hospital, as the days and weeks passed, I still had no idea how seriously injured I really was. I knew I couldn't see and I knew I couldn't feel my hands where the rocket had exploded. Things didn't get any clearer during the subsequent weeks in the hospital as my parents and the doctors hid the extent of my injuries. Although well-meaning in a cruel way, I was being misled. Daily.

"Well, you'll be able to do anything you could have done before," Mother regularly lied like any mother will, trying to "protect" me from the grim truth.

The reality of my medical situation was that I needed eight pints of blood just to survive. I'd lost one eye immediately in the explosion, but still had partial vision in my remaining eye. Then there were my hands, which were still a question mark for me, hidden deep in layers of red-stained gauze bandages.

One day when I went in for one of many surgeries, the doctors decided to sedate me with painkillers while keeping me conscious. They wanted to see how much mobility and feeling I had in my (remaining) fingers. I was conscious and I could see, not well, but well enough. As the doctors probed, prodded, and tested, I lifted my head a few inches off the pillow and peered down at my hands. Through the snow white, drugged haze, I saw the mangled mess that was left of my hands. I couldn't make out the difference between fingers and knuckles; where my hands ended and wrists began. I dropped my head back onto the pillow, certain that I had hallucinated the whole horrifying sight. Unfortunately, I had not.

DETACHED

After six weeks in the hospital and a couple dozen surgeries (possibly thirty, I lost count), it was time for me to return to life, my new normal. Even with one eye lost in the accident, my eyesight was good enough that I could drive a car; for short distances only, but adequately. There was one lingering caveat, however. Some of the residual shrapnel from the explosion that nearly made me bleed to death had also lodged itself behind the retina, threatening my one remaining eye. This is where I entered purgatory, living in limbo between what was and what might be, but had not yet been decided.

I was physically restricted to reduce the risk of the fragile retina detaching in my remaining eye. Other than the four trips from Salt Lake City to San Francisco Children's Hospital for eye surgeries, I was mainly restricted to home, learning to navigate the world with eyes that saw differently and hands that felt differently. It was the condition of my hands that upset me the most. I thought, "It would have been so much better if I'd been completely blinded instead of having such disfigured hands." Be careful what you wish for.

Purgatory (n): a place of temporary suffering or misery

Purgatory is a profoundly frustrating place to live. I don't recommend it at all if you can avoid it. My peers, now seniors in high school, were planning their lives. Whether that meant their Mormon missions or off to college, they enjoyed the gift of planning their futures. I couldn't plan for anything because nobody knew how the eye surgeries would turn out. Nothing could be resolved. I was at the complete mercy of my situation with no choices. Physically restricted, my mind took flight, moving back and forth, constantly between hope and fear.

"I'm not the person I was but I don't know who I'm going to be. Who will want me? Who will date me? Who will value me? Who will hire me?"

Most people never realize they're living in purgatory because it has seemed normal for so long. Because my version of purgatory was so pronounced and different, I was fully aware. And I wanted to crawl out of my skin the whole time.

Finally, what would be my last eye surgery happened in February of 1963, nine months after the rocket exploded in my hands and took out one of my eyes. Now, I lay in the hospital bed after the surgery with the "good" eye in postoperative bandages. Mother was perched anxiously on the edge of the bedside chair like a bird about to take flight. We were about to receive the verdict on my eyesight and my life moving forward. Father stayed back home in Salt Lake, running the candy factory while also working a part-time job to pay my medical bills.

I heard two doctors walk somberly into the room. I could sense their reluctance because they didn't come bustling in as usual, with the sounds and voice tones of regular daily business. This was different. They walked slowly. This was a conversation that neither wanted to have, especially in regards to a seventeen-year-old boy with his whole life ahead of him. And then…

"We have done all we can do. He will be blind for the rest of his life," one of the doctors said, speaking slowly, haltingly.

The other doctor stood beside him adjusting his stethoscope and fiddling nervously, but not saying a word.

The news the doctors delivered was an incredible relief after months of the unbearable tension of uncertainty, already completely blind in one eye from the explosion, wondering about the fate of the other eye where I still had partial eyesight. With the announcement of the verdict, the walls of purgatory came crashing to the ground and I finally felt *free*! Free to plan, to explore options, to take action, to move forward.

The surgeons, grabbed a box of tissues, handed it to my hysterical mother, and rushed out of the room. Surgeons don't historically have the best bedside manner and these two couldn't wait to get back into surgical scrubs and grab their scalpels.

The narrative they projected for me was bleak and powerless. This is understandable since blind people in 1963 had few options. I would basically be offered a guide dog, a collapsible stick, and the limiting label "disabled." I rejected not only this label, but also the entire narrative built around it.

How does a seventeen-year-old, especially one in a traumatic situation, make such a bold decision? I might not have, if my father hadn't spent six months at my bedside reading inspirational poems, books, and stories.

Even after all these years and experiences, successes and failures, I am often guided by the same quote from William Ernest Henley's poem *Invictus* that my father read to me. This quote helped push me to action in the very beginning days from my hospital bed.

> Out of the night that covers me,
> Black as the pit from pole to pole,
> I thank whatever gods may be
> For my unconquerable soul.
>
> In the fell clutch of circumstance
> I have not winced nor cried aloud.
> Under the bludgeonings of chance
> My head is bloody, but unbowed.

> Beyond this place of wrath and tears
> > Looms but the Horror of the shade,
> And yet the menace of the years
> > Finds and shall find me unafraid.

> It matters not how strait the gate,
> > How charged with punishments the scroll,
> I am the master of my fate,
> > I am the captain of my soul.

Left with my unglued, sobbing mother, I knew it was up to me, the teenager who'd just been benched in the game of life, to take action. It had been less than an hour since I was declared completely blind for life.

Mother was a legal secretary, so I thought that if I could occupy her mind with a familiar task, it might just bring her back in off the ledge.

"Mother, I want you to take a letter," I said.

She became silent and blinked at me in confusion for a moment. Then, almost by force of habit, she grabbed a notepad and wrote down what I said. This single task got her mind off the future. She was back in the present and taking "action."

The letter was to Guide Dogs for the Blind in San Rafael. It was an application to get a guide dog. I realized years later that by taking this action, I was making a declaration that would shape my life's story.

President Kennedy had made his space declaration just two years earlier, and so as a teenage boy in his garage in Salt Lake City, I fell in love with flight. I became enamored with the Space Race, but unfortunately was no rocket scientist.

But now, lying in that hospital bed, vowing to take action to change the course of my life, I felt connected to the president's passion for freeing oneself from limitations and finding a way to fly. In my case, I would be flying blind. I vowed not to let it stop me from living a life that I defined—not one decided by others.

CHAPTER 2
ROBBING BANKS

I n a world where all too often people are more inclined to pop a happy pill to quell nerves or depressed thoughts, or suppress mental or physical pain, the power of taking action is often overlooked. Action always produces a better mood. It's inaction and inactivity that are painful. For instance, there was the pain of the enforced boredom of purgatory while I waited for the verdict on my eyesight. I suppose I could have asked for some sort of prescription-grade remedy rather than endure the daily battle of wanting to crawl out of my skin. Ironically, it wasn't until later on after the diagnosis following my final eye surgery of "there's nothing else we can do for you" that Mother and the doctors thought I should see a psychiatrist to "process" what had happened. Feeling nothing but relief at the opportunity to finally leave purgatory and get on with my life, I thought they were the crazy ones for suggesting such a thing. Receiving my prognosis relieved the torture of inactivity, anxiety of uncertainty, and the depression of boredom all in one fell swoop.

With Mother's grief at bay for the time being, I could focus on my own declarations for the future. Granted, back in the San Francisco Children's Hospital in 1963, I didn't call these thoughts and actions I was having "declarations." And I certainly did not know these declarations were a crucial tool to shift my narrative. I just knew that I was identifying what I wouldn't tolerate about my life. This closed some possibilities while opening the door for others. The actions I would take would be designed to support the possibilities that remained.

One day later, with nothing more that could be done for me, Mother and I headed back home to Salt Lake City. Other than my eyesight, I was a perfectly healthy teenage boy who still had one year of high school to complete.

Word had spread quickly about my prognosis. When our plane touched down, most of the family had gathered at the airport, waiting to see me. There was Father, my brother, and aunts and uncles including Uncle Jake.

More so than my blindness, I was still self-conscious about my left hand, which was mostly missing. While in California, we purchased a cosmetic prosthesis that slid on like a glove over what remained of my hand, and looked like a full left hand. Mother and I emerged from the flight ramp into the airport with an airline employee pushing me in a wheelchair. I found this odd since there was nothing at all wrong with my legs. Back then, as now, that's how blind people are treated. Disabled is disabled for many who don't see a difference.

I arranged my hands in my lap in a resting position, with the plastic left one stacked over the real right one. This position also intentionally concealed the missing thumb and index finger on my right hand. My Uncle Vern, even though he knew the condition of my hands, was impressed with the display. I think he was also comforted, protected from the jarring sight of my actual hands. This was more comfortable for everyone.

"Oh, he has a really nice way of holding his hands now," Uncle Vern commented.

He didn't realize I was wearing the prosthesis but could tell something was different. I was amused, but ultimately only ended up wearing the thing for a year before deciding it was really unnecessary.

It was early spring and guide dog school wouldn't come until after graduation, so it was back to high school for me a few days after getting home. Once again, I was relieved and almost jubilant to have purposeful actions—go back to school, attend class, study, take exams, and finish high school. I was also thrilled to be someplace other than in a hospital with Mother after the five eye surgeries in San Francisco over the past few months.

My classmates had only gotten a brief glimpse of me after the accident. I went back to school for about ten days back in August. A prosthetic eye replaced the one I'd lost in the explosion. My remaining eye, which still had some vision, was obscured behind thick coke bottle glasses so heavy that they had to be hooked behind my ears to stay up. "Some vision" is being very generous since my vision was 20/400 with 20/200 being legally blind. I navigated the crowded, chaotic hallways with a cane, leaving class early to avoid the rush.

That was before I was put in medical seclusion from September until February to protect my good eye from jarring itself. I was a different person now, about to reenter the seeing world. My declaration that I would not be poor, unmarriageable, homebound, helpless or "disabled" would soon be put to the test.

One thing happened right away that added fuel to my declaration. I didn't have a guide dog yet and I was in no way proficient in cane travel. I found myself feeling my way along walls, lockers, and around doorways, clumsily tapping my cane on any obstacle in my path, trying to figure out what it was. If the object moved and turned out to be a living being, I had to remember to stop hitting it; that kind of thing wouldn't make me popular with people. Navigating this way, essentially trying not to fall over and end up sprawled on a hallway floor as road kill, was difficult enough with no one around. But when the bell rang at my 2,700-student high school, the hallways became bustling subway tunnels, with swarms of sighted students flowing like a fast moving riptide in every possible direction. I was afraid I'd get swept up and unceremoniously spit out into the parking lot. To avoid this, the academic powers-that-be granted me permission to leave my classes five minutes early so I could get to my next destination before the subway tunnel filled with rowdy students. I also didn't want to resort to walking around on the elbow of an escort; that clearly went against my declaration to not be dependent on others.

Well, the thing that happened that fueled my declaration happened one day when I was hugging the wall, tapping awkwardly away, en route to my next class. I walked by two janitors who clearly thought I couldn't hear them. Perhaps blind and deaf went hand in hand to them.

"Isn't that the most pitiful thing you've ever seen?" one janitor said to the other.

Listening, to my fragile ego, it felt like they were also thinking that everyone would be better off had I died and not been such a burden.

I don't think they were intentionally being unkind. This simply reflected the attitude of people at the time and they were just going with the current thought without questioning it. This is understandable since many people today are still drifting in their stories without resisting or asking questions. I understood that. But I still took it personally and it added fuel to my fire of personal independence. I also saw that I wasn't alone in this distinction, being seen as "out of the game" by many. This thinking isn't limited to the disabled.

You're the wrong color. You're in the wrong club. You're not playing our game. You're out of it.

Even my friends were affected by this thinking. Since the accident, things got awkward and they basically divided themselves into two groups: the few who moved closer, and the majority who drifted away. We were moving speedily toward graduation day and people were making their plans. Most were going to college, with the biggest percentage defaulting to the local University of Utah. A small number were heading to out-of-state schools. Some were fellow Mormons going on a mission for the LDS church.

I was raised as a Mormon and there's a presumption that at age nineteen, male church members will go on what used to be a thirty-month mission, often to a foreign country. These missionaries are supported by their families or their church flock, and the missionaries receive no compensation. Some of them live in pretty humble conditions. One friend who was on that path, automatically assumed that I would be disappointed about not going. Quite honestly, it hadn't called to me in any way to do that; I had enough trouble tapping around the school hallways let alone trying to navigate my way around a foreign country. I had no regrets whatsoever.

My plan was, and had always been, to go on to college. I knew that without education and skills, I would be condemned to welfare, unemployment, and dependency. This is what would make me a disabled citizen, I decided, not my lack of physical eyesight. My mother on the other hand, had already decided that I would never be able to leave home and never be able to marry.

Remember, I still wasn't thinking of these beliefs that were forming, as "declarations fueled by action that are the tools needed to shape my life narrative." I was just thinking of what I needed to do, and what I needed to not do.

I was also thinking from the standpoint of proving people wrong who saw me from their preconceived "disabled" attitudes.

WHERE THE MONEY IS

Once I had my high school diploma, the next step was college. This was another pretty easy step since the University of Utah had a requirement to accept all in-state residents. It was a low-cost university to begin with, plus I was on welfare, which paid for the education. This is possibly the only smart use for welfare—education. The other uses of the program make you promise to stay in purgatory no matter what; to not work, not save, not invest, and not marry the father of your children. These three things alone are guaranteed to destroy a life.

A declaration always opens and closes possibilities. If your declaration, like mine, is to be independent, the possibility of goofing off at the beach all year is inconsistent and therefore ruled out. Or, using welfare money to stay unemployed, stay home, and stay stupid, are also all ruled out. Once enough possibilities are ruled out, we arrive at actions consistent with the declaration. Get into the University of Utah. Live at home. Go to school. Get a degree. Get skills that will be valued. The last one helped me choose a major. Many students go about choosing a major from all the possibilities. I went in reverse, using process of elimination. By stating, "Get skills that will be valued," I immediately ruled out dozens of majors. So I didn't major in gender studies, for instance. I'm joking a little since that wasn't offered back then, but you get the idea. My declaration had me rule out the "no job degrees" in favor of the "job degrees." I chose banking, finance, accounting, and most of all, economics. As the notorious bank robber Willie Sutton said when asked why he robbed banks, "Because that's where the money is!" So, I studied banking and finance because of the money.

This also solved some of the social challenges of college, like popularity. Remember that in high school I was a mediocre student at best, never the "braniac" of any group. Now, at the University of Utah, in a serious major and powered by the declaration to get new skills and a good job (plus a date), I became a valuable social commodity to some of the other students. As a freshman, I was quickly recruited into a fraternity so my frat brothers could continue to party while my 4.0 GPA brought up the house average, thereby keeping the party going. Rather than feeling used, I enjoyed this turn of events as "good student." It was like going from being the kid picked last at pickup baseball to the one picked first. I didn't do things bad students do because it didn't fit my new narrative. The strength of my declaration and focus on succeeding no matter what, transformed me from a bottom of the class high school student to graduating first in my class. Grades aren't everything; as you may know a famous Civil War general graduated last in his class at West Point. On the other hand, those who argue that grades predict success are first to remind us that general was George Armstrong Custer.

Beyond that, this new path, via college into an investment career, required a complete change of my previous life narrative. I no longer assumed I would just drift into the family business and take over. As a result of that day in the hospital, my answer to the question "who are you?" and thus my life narrative, had been rewritten. When I was told I would be blind forever, I realized that I would not be taking over the family's candy business and that I needed to prepare myself for a different life than I had assumed.

CHAPTER 3
OUT OF THE DARKNESS

Within an hour of finding out that I would never see again, I took action. I dictated a letter to my mother to apply for admission to a guide dog school in San Rafael. If I couldn't see my way through the independent, prosperous life I desired, I would need a companion who could guide me. This is when I started putting this declaration, to never be dependent on others, into action. That summer after high school graduation, my friends celebrated and prepared for college or their Mormon missions, I went back to school, or as I called it, going to meet my new best friend of the four-legged variety.

The guide dog school was free, supported by contributions and endowments. It was started after World War II by a U.S. Army canine corps officer to train dogs for blind veterans. The buildings were old

World War II era, temporarily built wooden structures that sat on about sixteen to twenty acres.

The curriculum ran for twenty-eight days, many of which were spent sitting around and waiting. It was three or four days before we even got our dogs. That's when students got to know one another. There were fifteen students, divided into two basic categories, those who were born blind and those who had once been sighted. A lot of the blind population in the early 1960s were incubator babies whose eyes had been damaged by excessive oxygen as preemies. The other group was older people who were blind from age-related optical issues. I was the only one who had lost eyesight from trauma; I tended to hang out with the people who had once been sighted as we had more in common.

The anticipation of getting our dogs, which didn't happen until around day four, built. I felt like I was in limbo again, desperately wanting to take action. Bring on the next step in the journey of my life! My family had a dog growing up, and while I understand that all living creatures are special, our dog in Salt Lake City was very un-special. It was untrained and had few requirements beyond feeding it, walking it, and cleaning up after it. I was curious to find out how a trained "professional" dog would be different.

They trained us on the basics of guide dog care and performed examinations to test our stamina, walking speed, and mobility. I got more and more impatient with all the pre-training. I wondered what breed of dog I would get, the name, and the gender. I was like a kid counting down the days until Christmas! Finally, they brought me the key to my mobility. Her name was Minka and she was a small sixty-five pound female German shepherd.

The guide dogs were already about ninety percent trained, which is a very high standard. So the first day was spent getting to know our dogs. I quickly made a pact with Minka to figure out this whole new partnership together and we shook on it.

Minka was a funny one. She thought that if she couldn't see other people, they couldn't see her. She would hide her head behind a telephone pole and think that her whole body was hidden, the way an ostrich puts his head in the ground and thinks it's hidden. She of course didn't understand what "blind" was either, but she did learn as part of her training that if she didn't get out of the way, I would step on her (versus the other humans who would step over her).

Once we became acquainted it was time to go on our very first walk together. It was morning, the sun had just come up and the air was so pure. I could smell the dew. I finally had my legs back and was ready for my newfound freedom. The moment that Minka and I took our first steps together I felt reborn. It was like the line from *Oliver*, "I now know how it feels to fly through the streets with wings on my heels." It was the first time, since losing my eyesight the year before, that I could walk at a rapid pace without fear of falling and without being pushed and pulled by a sighted person who had no idea how to lead a blind person. I was a free man again!

One thing we were drilled on in the guide school was to always follow your dog. Do not disagree with your dog because most of the time (as in ninety-nine percent) she will be right. If you disobey your dog, you may fall in a trench. They know what you're doing and you do not. We were taught this repeatedly and I thought I'd listened.

Minka and I practiced all over San Rafael and then San Francisco, navigating sidewalks, crosswalks, local stores, elevators, escalators, bus rides, and busy city environments. I obediently let Minka take the lead and she never led me wrong, until we got back home to Salt Lake City. That's when my ego took charge as I walked very quickly around the streets where I'd grown up. Suddenly Minka came to an abrupt stop and would not budge. I urged her forward, corrected her, and finally got her to step ahead. Whack! I ran right into the low branch of a tree. She was doing her job but I wasn't doing mine! Minka and I would continue to have our adventures together over the years. This was a whole new world based on one single declaration of independence and I was determined to learn to navigate.

CHAPTER 4

REJECTION

> *If the rule you followed brought you to this,*
> *of what use was the rule?*
> —**Cormac McCarthy**, No Country for Old Men

1967

My hospital bed "declarations" were:

I will not be poor.
I will not be dependent on others.
I will not live at home, be led to the bathroom, fed, and walked.
I will live an active, independent life and be valued by people.

23

All of these would require getting a job.

I'd just graduated first in my class from the University of Utah. In the career world of banking and finance, this meant I had a diploma from an undistinguished university in the western mountains. I realized this wouldn't be good enough for the successful career I envisioned. My job prospects weren't great. I needed more skills and credentials and knew that the "hot degree" at the time was an MBA.

Next declaration: I will get an MBA from a prestigious university.

As with any declaration, it needed to be immediately accompanied by "action." MBAs don't fall out of the sky. So I applied to Harvard and Stanford. Stanford accepted and processed my application and my $25 check before letting me know that a blind person would not be able to graduate from their school. Twenty-five dollars might not seem like a lot of money now, but it was one hundred gallons of gasoline at the time, a lot for a student on welfare. Harvard, being better endowed, at least sent the check back when they came to the same conclusion.

How could either school know that a blind person couldn't graduate from their MBA program if neither had actually admitted anyone who was blind? Although their declarations lacked logic, their authority to make them valid supported the decisions.

I will get an MBA from a prestigious university.

So I rallied my friends, family, and other contacts, and organized a letter writing campaign to Stanford, where I thought my chances were better and where I preferred to go. This resulted in an outpouring of support from professors and students. One student even crafted a well-articulated challenge letter to the Stanford powers-that-be stating, "I have to wonder why Stanford feels it isn't up to the challenge of educating someone who is blind." The pressure continued by one of Stanford's alumni donors, the eponymous O.C. Tanner, founder of the well-known Utah jewelry company. Stanford did end up reconsidering my application and this time reached a different conclusion.

"We are now convinced that we were wrong; that you could graduate from our program. But it's our responsibility not to waste one of our slots on someone who is obviously unemployable," they wrote.

Even with my modest education and lack of eyesight, there was one thing I knew for sure about myself—I was much more than a wasted slot.

Keep in mind that this unfolded prior to the Higher Education Act of 1965, which legally prevented such discrimination. It was a time when things were much more clear and authentic than they are now. Stanford and Harvard wouldn't legally be able to refuse me today. Is this progress? As much as the rejections stung at the time, I don't think so. No matter what their biases, both schools were declaring their honest assessment of my chances at success in their programs. I wish I had had this very wise, levelheaded perspective back then.

The resounding "no's" were a big setback from my declaration, but I needed to take the next action and keep moving forward.

I will get an MBA from a prestigious university.

So I asked the question, "Which is the number three school?" It was the University of Pennsylvania's Wharton School of Business. Incidentally, I also had a number four school lined up and would find number five, six and so on if that's what it took to make good on my declaration. As the saying goes, "When Plan A doesn't work out, keep going because there are twenty-five other letters in the alphabet." There was never a thought of, "Oh well, got rejected, might as well go work in the family business." That action would be inconsistent with the declaration that I would get an MBA from a prestigious university. When the odds are against you and obstacles being thrown from many directions, having strong, clear declarations is what makes giving up on your narrative shift, impossible. It closes the loopholes that allow you to slip slide away from the design of your life.

Wharton met the requirement since the declaration was not to specifically go to Harvard or Stanford. There is a lesson here when you're writing your own declarations. Make the wording specific enough to prompt clear, focused action, but not so narrow that it closes too many possibilities and makes failure inevitable. There is only one Harvard, so if my declaration was, "I will get an MBA from Harvard," that foot race would have been over pretty quickly.

Not yet accepted but also not rejected, I took the long train ride from Salt Lake City to Philadelphia to meet with Wharton's Dean of Admissions, Dr. Blanchard. His declaration started the same as the others, but then it veered in a different direction.

"Well, I don't know if you can make it here or not because we've never admitted a person who is blind to our school," he said.

I wondered about the purpose of the long cross-country train ride east.

"But you're admitted anyway. I'm not even going to take this to the committee. You're admitted, and if you can't make it here, you'll have to leave."

That seemed fair enough, and we shook hands. It took persistence, but I produced the intersection where an available opportunity aligned with my declaration, so I was now able to move forward with my narrative. You need to produce those "intersections" in your own life. Years later I would found an investment company called Kairos Capital Advisors, the word Kairos a Greek word meaning, "That moment when vision, bold action and opportunity converge to achieve extraordinary accomplishment."

IN THE GAME

Now that I was becoming equipped with skills, my next declaration was: I will get a job in the investment business.

Once again I put myself near the top of my class, this time in the number five spot. Mother wanted to know whom the other four were. Perhaps behind every successful man there is an "unsatisfiable" mother.

As graduation neared, and my classmates were showered with job offers, usually multiple ones, Stanford started appearing correct. I could not get a job. Meanwhile, my peers would have four or five interviews and get three offers. Some got offers, usually from second-tier consulting or banking firms, even without the interview. Many received substantial signing bonuses. I couldn't even get a bite from the federal government. I had forty-nine job interviews and not a single offer.

Fear suddenly grabbed ahold of me. Just the word "unemployed" created images of welfare, homelessness, and moving back home to live with my parents. The mere thought haunted me at night. This was an unacceptable narrative with no connection to my declarations. I would keep looking for a job until I got one. That was the only possibility.

I will get a job in the investment business.

Then, a serendipitous connection turned things around. My classmate Robert Arthur received an offer from Cooke & Bieler, a tiny investment-counseling firm in Philadelphia.

Robert was hoping to bring me along with him to Cooke & Bieler. The problem was that it was only a six-professional firm and that year they'd already hired two new MBAs, their quota. They didn't want a third one. But because of Robert's high praise for me, they agreed to an interview. I met with one of the partners, Jim McLennan. Much to my surprise they made me an offer! It was a conditional offer similar to Wharton's, "We don't know if this will work but we're willing to try and if it doesn't you'll have to leave." That was more than good enough for me. I had a job in the investment business.

My responsibilities at Cooke & Bieler in the beginning included research-based security analyses of companies and their stocks, writing reports, making presentations and managing client portfolios as the junior person on client account teams. As a team we would do travel research, visit companies at their headquarters, interview the management, analyze financials and the industry, and reach conclusions as to what to buy and up to what price. It was all entry-level work and I dug in with a ferocious work ethic, learning as much as I could and determined to attain great success in this profession.

As a final, more serious point of interest in this story, the "conditional" offer that got me in the door at Cooke & Bieler, would be completely illegal after The Americans with Disabilities Act passed in 1990. The firm would have been guilty of illegal discrimination since they didn't make "reasonable accommodation" as that law requires. For example, in my case, "reasonable accommodation" might include modifications to the workplace so I could navigate "safely and without harm," modifying office equipment so I could use it, or providing a reader to help me do my work. This is one reason, in my opinion, that the unemployment rate for the seriously disabled has increased so much since the ADA was passed. It precludes companies from doing what Cooke & Bieler did, offer someone a chance, which puts the employer in jeopardy. The jeopardy comes not from trying to skirt special accommodations rules (which Cooke & Bieler never attempted to do), but because no business wants to take a chance on an employee that they cannot terminate if necessary. It is simply not a smart business practice.

Employers are put at risk whenever they hire a member of any "protected class." The only thing that members of the class are protected from is being employed! With the ADA, Cooke & Bieler would have said (amongst each other in private of course), "Are you crazy? We already hired two MBAs and you want us to hire a third who's fire proof?" But without it, fortunately, I was in.

CONGRESSIONAL COMPASS

Having worked my way up from analyst to portfolio manager to Chief Investment Officer, by the early 1970s, I was a partner at Cooke & Bieler. During my time there I had the honor of being mentored in finance by one of the greatest economic thinkers of our time, Art Laffer, creator of the "Laffer Curve." Art's story began back in the mid-1970s when the world was in a state of economic confusion and turmoil. In 1974, Art dined in Washington D.C. with Dick Cheney, Donald Rumsfeld, and political economist Jude Wanniski. By the main course, Art found himself unsuccessfully trying to explain a new economic concept he'd been working on that he called the Laffer Curve. So he grabbed one of the linen napkins from the table of the upscale restaurant, asked the waiter for a sharpie marker, and drew a picture of the curve.

I became a fan of the Laffer Curve, and brought the supply-side economics story right through the front doors of Cooke & Bieler by bringing Art on as an advisor. Some of my associates were skeptical at such a wild economic theory, but I stood firm. One of the first things I did was take Art out to lunch at a local Japanese sushi restaurant on the same block as the firm, and shamelessly asked him to recreate the "dinner napkin." There, in the midst of the slicing of raw fish, Art obliged. He found a linen napkin and drew his diagram, describing to me what he was sketching. I have that napkin today, framed on a wall in my house.

One axis of the inverted U shaped curve represents tax rates, and the other, tax revenues. The curve shows that there are two tax rates that will produce exactly the same revenues—the zero tax rate will produce zero revenues, and the hundred percent tax rate will also produce zero revenues. Many believe that this idea where tax rates actually matter and lowering tax rates could increase revenue, was pretty wacky. But it caught on and history has proven its merit; and as a parallel, it's also the reason that when stores have sales, it often increases their revenue. Lower prices can result in higher overall revenue.

The Laffer Curve became a big influencer of government economic policy and I had a front row seat observing the intersection of policy and investing. This new narrative of how government policies not only direct economies but set global asset prices became a powerful one in my life.

Understanding the power of policy, particularly monetary and tax policy, I wanted badly to be appointed to the Federal Reserve Board. I shamelessly admit that this opportunity only existed in the first place because Uncle Jake was a U.S. Senator and also chair of the Senate Banking Committee. Jake went to the Senate Majority Leader at the time, Bob Dole, to see about an appointment for me. Senator Dole had just appointed another person and didn't want to push his privilege such a short time later. This was disappointing to me, but Senator Dole came back with a different idea of how I could get into the government influence game.

"What I do want you to do, and I would consider it a personal favor, is to be on the U.S. Civil Rights Commission. I have the power of appointment this year. I want to appoint someone who is disabled, but doesn't make a living from being disabled," said Senator Dole, in his matter-of-fact Midwestern way.

Bob Dole was disabled himself. In World War II he was in the 10th Mountain Division, a ski-based fighting unit in the Italian Alps. He took a bullet in his right hand and arm and was permanently disabled as a result.

There was only one way for me to respond.

"Senator Dole, I am honored and I accept."

It was a part-time job and I didn't have to leave my investment partnership in Philadelphia. I would serve about forty hours a month on the commission, taking a short train down to the Capitol for a day or two each month. We also had investigative field trips and the power to subpoena documents and witnesses. I was now in Washington about to begin affecting policy.

I quickly learned the harsh realties of causing real change in Washington D.C. Like many things in our government, the Civil Rights Commission is designed in a way that doesn't allow it to accomplish much. You see, there are eight commissioners, the perfect formula for a maddening record of ties and deadlocked decisions. It's a poor design, and I fully credit the government for having planned it.

The commission was designed in 1958 by the Eisenhower administration and quickly descended into political football, with the Left sometimes controlling the game and the Right at other times. The ball would get passed from one side to the other, and the game would continue with no real winner or progress made.

For me, one of the more productive things that came from serving on the commission was learning how to write dissents. These are the official opinions of the Civil Rights Commission on various national situations; like, for instance the presidential election of 2000.

Commissioner Abby Thernstrom and I were commissioned to write the dissent against those who concluded that President Bush Jr. stole the election in Florida. We ended up with a fifty-four-page dissent, which is normally far too long, but in many ways, so was the entire situation itself. The specific allegation our report addressed was that Catherine Harris, the Secretary of State of Florida responsible for supervising elections, somehow conspired with twenty different county commissioners including a great many Democrats to rig Florida's presidential vote. They produced no evidence to support this claim, by the way. One point that I brought up was how difficult it was to get volunteers to become good at anything they do only once every four years. If the allegations were true this was indeed a masterful scheme by highly intelligent, skilled individuals. I'm not sure if that kind of personal wit made it into the report since the final drafts were more courtroom style than cable news commentary. We hired some experts on voting statistics and included a powerful statistical refutation to support our position.

The final dissent expanded to seventy-one pages. We used statistical methods to demonstrate that the outcome of the election was absolutely consistent with the voting patterns and that there wasn't any improper influence by Catherine Harris, especially on the many Democratic country commissioners who would have needed to cooperate. There was a lot of testimony stating otherwise, but testimony is not evidence. Consistent with my viewpoint of the world as an economist, we used evidence.

With Bush "43" securely in office, but still under Democrat domination in Congress, the next hallmark in my stint on the Civil Rights Commission came when we identified some funny stuff going on with money. It was actually not funny at all, but rather criminal; missing money and money spent on things that were not appropriate. There was an obvious love relationship accompanied by a financial arrangement between one important commissioner and one important staff member.

Those of us in the minority on the commission demanded an audit to find out what happened to the money. I led a group to reorganize the entire commission and clean up all the abuses, after it became clear that the Republicans would come into control the next year. It was clear that we would finally have the majority and be free to make important changes, but I wanted the changes to be agreed upon by both Democrats and Republicans. I'd learned in business by then, that "win-win" agreements are historically more successful and permanent than when one side bullies the other.

Let's be clear that this wasn't a political problem I was trying to fix, but an organizational design problem. It was a redesign of the organization to make it more transparent, authentic, and effective. As expected, I got a lot of pushback from the Democrats. But to my surprise, I received an equal amount of objection from the incoming Republicans. I quickly realized that what was happening was even more criminal than I thought.

The thinking by some of the Republicans on the commission seemed to be, "You don't understand. It's going to be our turn soon, and then we can do the same things. We can exert the same power. But if your reforms are adopted, Russell, none of it will be allowed." This all became clear to me as I testified before the Committee of Congress regarding the flaws in our group. I recommended that Congress suspend, defund, and eliminate the Civil Rights Commission. I told them they had the power to kill the commission and that's what they should do.

This wasn't an impossible idea. President Reagan closed several agencies with bipartisan support (not nearly as many as he promised he would, but he did eliminate entire agencies). But in this case they couldn't get that bipartisan agreement, and neither party wants to be attached to the headline that they "killed the Civil Rights Commission." The challenge I laid down for them was too big of a risk and was rejected by both sides.

Following my declaration that serving on the commission wasn't something I was willing to tolerate under these circumstances, I quit. I couldn't see how to possibly stay. I wasn't being resentful or punitive. There was no blaming of certain individuals or anything like that. I was just stating the facts. "This is clearly not working. Here are the things you need to do. Either close it or do these things, either way, I'm gone." As a side note, it occurs to me that since I was on the commission for fifteen years, either I gave them plenty of time to change, or I'm a very slow learner.

If you'd like to read the media coverage of my resignation, I'd suggest you search on the Internet, "Russell Redenbaugh quits Civil Rights Commission." You'll get quite an eyeful and hopefully in some way my opinions will provide some insights into the inner workings of our government policymakers. It is scary to realize that these policy shenanigans not only happen in the small rooms of Civil Rights Commissions but in dealings that affect the growth of our eighteen trillion dollar economy and the prosperity of our 350 million citizens.

I left Washington fully aware of the power of policy and what it meant for investors. This policy-based investing narrative is not one

Wall Street likes, but it is one that I would successfully rely on many times over my investing career.

My civil rights experience also demonstrates the importance of making decisions based on your own "north star." Have you ever been put in a position that you innately knew went against your beliefs and declarations? How did that feel? Most likely you felt a sense of discomfort, which came from your beliefs being out of alignment with your circumstances. This is one reason of many why declarations are important in your life. If you haven't clearly established what you will and will not accept, how will you be able to identify situations where a decision must be made?

THE BIGGEST SHIFT

By the mid-1980s, the Soviet Union was on the brink of collapse and I saw big possibilities on the horizon for the United States, especially from an investment standpoint. At Cooke & Bieler, we had been running the business in a way that was appropriate as long as the "evil empire" stood and the Cold War was not yet won. Then, when the Soviet Union disappeared almost overnight, there was talk of a "peace dividend." My partners argued that the dividend wouldn't be that great because military spending could not drop very much. They were thinking like accountants, and they were right in terms of accounting. I argued that the peace dividend had much larger implications. Beyond lower spending, the peace dividend also meant there was no longer a threat of nuclear annihilation. The removal of that threat, I predicted, had a high value in financial markets. It would be a positive factor for income, output, employment, and stock prices for decades.

I found myself at odds with my partners at Cooke & Bieler around the very issue I had been learning since my hospital bed, narratives matter. Investors live in narratives about the present and the future, a future that is expected to be either better or worse. These narratives can dramatically alter asset valuations and affect market prices. The end of the Cold War produced a boom in the general economy and in technology specifically. The narrative my partners were missing, but I was seeing, was that the end of the Soviet Union would unleash freedom, opportunity, and prosperity around the globe and I believed the stock market would "notice." I ended up being correct; in response to better economic policies US stocks advanced 1,400% in the 1980s and 1990s (a $1 million portfolio grew to $14 million). Having the right narrative can make and save you a lot of money. The narrative disagreement caused me to turn my sights to opportunities beyond Cooke & Bieler.

Also as the Soviet Union was falling, Silicon Valley was rising. I had been spending more and more time in California analyzing technology companies for Cooke & Bieler. I'd also become a student of Dr. Fernando Flores, who owned a software company dedicated to making corporations more efficient. He had an email-based program designed to improve action, project coordination, and completion in a business setting.

The more time I spent immersed in the future on the west coast, the more uninspiring it became to go back east to continuing investment narrative conflict. I felt like a racehorse in a traffic jam.

My partners at Cooke & Bieler were buried in leather-bound financial prospectuses based on incorrect assessments about the new post-Cold War investment landscape, while Dr. Flores was surfing the information superhighway, cracking codes to revolutionize corporate America. One was not more correct than the other; they were just two different worlds for me. I knew where I wanted to be.

It was time for a new narrative and thus a new declaration to set me on the path toward it. I will become a technology investor/consultant.

Next was the matter of taking actions that supported my new declaration. I needed a job in technology. Studying with Dr. Flores and helping him with his business, I let it be known that I was available for another career opportunity if he knew of anything. He promptly made me an offer to be CEO of his software company.

This decision had big risks. There was the fact that I was walking away from a shockingly high income, I had no idea if I was doing the right thing, and the software industry was very new to me. But I felt like if it wasn't now it would certainly be never.

The universe tends to oppose bold declarations. But that didn't mean the world was going to throw me a ticker tape parade in honor of my courage. It doesn't work that way. The first person who wasn't celebrating, of course, was Mother. Even though I was financially successful, her mind went back to my accident. She immediately became terrified about my financial future, convinced I would end up broke and dependent on her.

However, I knew going into this that my biggest obstacle by far would be breaking away from Cooke & Bieler. I was locked into both an employment contract as well a non-compete agreement with the owners (although I wasn't leaving to compete against them). I was also the largest revenue producer in the firm, had the heaviest client load, and the largest share of the fees compared to any other partners. They were not happy at all. For them, this was a lightning bolt coming down on a sunny, otherwise peaceful day, and splitting a tree in half. I'd just shaken up their world with no warning. There was anger ("Who do you think you are anyway?"), self-righteousness ("How dare you, you have a contract!") and other completely normal emotions for such a situation. When one person makes a dramatic life shift, the ripple effects shake up others involved. This certainly doesn't make one party right and the other wrong.

Ultimately, beyond simply standing my ground and refusing to reverse my decision, I made a deal with Cooke & Bieler to leave quietly (versus making it a matter of public record) and agreed to completely honor my non-compete in the investment business. It was the big shift that in the end happened with a whisper. I did not leave for a competitor, but for a different life.

I broke free and headed west, like early American pioneers. They weren't entirely sure what they were looking for or what was going to happen, but like me, weren't interested in sticking around back east either. The vast majority didn't move for gold; they moved for a better life. They were restless for change, freedom, and new opportunities. So was I.

Beyond shifting my job and my geography, the massive narrative shift from Cooke & Bieler to Silicon Valley shifted my habits, my outlook on life, even my social friends. The biggest, most effective shifts in life do that—it's never just about "the decision." When a shift is truly tectonic (vs. "life changes"), your entire ecosystem changes and nothing looks like it used to.

But the fact was, leaving Cooke & Bieler in the late 1980s was the last time in my life in which I had a paycheck. There would be times I would miss that.

SOFTWARE FAIL

We learn more from our failures than from our victories.
—Russell Redenbaugh

I now found myself as CEO of Action Technologies, a software company in Silicon Valley. Settling into my glass-walled corner office, overlooking other hungry, young technology startups, I wondered if I was born to innovate after all.

We were working in a rarified environment at Action Technologies with top PhDs in Computer Science, including Terry Winograd, who is considered the father of artificial intelligence. Terry was a full professor at Stanford at twenty-four years old. I myself was even named as co-inventor on two of our patents. I was now initiated into a membership club of bona fide technological geniuses. It was a miracle that they'd have me.

Our product, a combination of project management and email, was very far ahead of its time. Email is almost considered ancient technology now, but in the 1980s, it was extremely rare, and to most people in business, a mystery. It had been around longer for larger entities like the government and university systems, but existed on large mainframes versus personal email on a personal computer.

For the most part, the people of corporate America were still photocopying memos, sending faxes, and picking up landlines to reach out and touch someone. AOL had only just appeared and we were all just getting used to their once familiar musical modems. Yahoo! was so new that people were still figuring out how to categorize it. Was it a search engine portal or some type of low-grade email? The Internet was in its infancy, and its customers were taking baby steps, hugging the couch, trying not to fall down, and trying to navigate unfamiliar territory.

So we decided to fly a complicated time machine right through the center of Silicon Valley. As it turns out, this wasn't the smartest business idea. There's a difference between being ahead of your time, and being so far ahead that people have no idea what you're talking about.

Our product was very complicated and technologically sophisticated. Yes, it was a DOS product because Microsoft Windows wasn't out yet. Everything showed up in little windows on the screen. It was very primitive, but in terms of functionality, it was ahead of the curve.

It not only was ahead of its time but it was also the wrong product for the people and processes of that time. A combination of email and project management, our software tracked requests, promises, and completions within a company. You could create and sort a database based on what deadlines and tasks were coming up, what was overdue and by how much. You could slice it up in many different ways based on the information you were looking for. It performed these tasks very vigorously. So much so, in fact, that one of our critics called it "Naziware." This, of course, was not our intent.

The software was based on flaws in human nature, where only a small percentage of people have excellent practices for managing their commitments, deadlines, emails, and follow through. The idea with this product was that you didn't need to be perfect in your practices. If you used this software, it would guide you into tracking commitments that you made to people and vice versa. As far as we were concerned, it fixed the procrastination error in human mental software.

People didn't like it. OK, people *hated* it! One of many things I learned from the experience is how much people loath saying "I promise" about anything. You can have the world's best, most airtight systems in place, but as long as we humans are around, there is always the possibility of things going off the rails.

The unfortunate part, especially for our investors and our financials, was that we were all true believers. We were drinking the Kool-Aid by the gallon. We thought this was the greatest product in the entire Bay Area if not the world. Looking back, I think the reason we thought this was because we were all the kind of people who didn't need this software. It was the disorganized masses we were out to save.

Unlike the fast burn of the gunpowder in my homemade rocket, failure is a slow burn. Success and failure do not normally happen overnight. While the scientists worked on improving the product and the sales guys peddled it to corporations, it was my job as CEO to raise the money to keep us all in business.

I raised money in two different rounds, selling shares to angel investors, and doing whatever else I could to bring in funding. Nothing was working.

Then I found a friend and professional investor, Bill Welty, to put in money and join our board. He quit his professional investing job, and ultimately became a full-time executive. The truth was self-evident and everyone agreed when I recommended that we find somebody who was better at being a software CEO than me. I quit and stayed on the board. Nevertheless, several years after I left, the company went down swinging into the Silicon Valley graveyard of failed startups.

It was a huge risk, leaving the financial and career security of Cooke & Bieler for the fast-paced excitement of Silicon Valley. There have been times when I thought the decision was a mistake, walking away from the money and security of the financial world. But it was not a mistake. There are few lessons in easy victories.

CHAPTER 5
PINNING GOLIATH

P eriodically throughout my life I discovered additional narratives I wanted to shift. Of course this meant new declarations and actions needed to make these shifts. From the shock of the blindness verdict in my teens, the uphill academic climb out of welfare toward wealth in my twenties, working at Cooke & Bieler and then in Silicon Valley in my thirties, and in my forties returning back to the investment advisory business—the next "big shift" that I would make was a personal, not professional one.

One day, when I was working out at the gym with my fitness coach, Steve Maxwell, he said, "Russell I have a plan for you. I want you to become my client. I know you go to work early so I'll come by at 5:30 every morning and we'll go for a jog. Then we'll end up back at the gym, lift some weights, and then I'll bring you back home so you can get showered up and go to work."

I absorbed all this and realized something.

"Wait a minute, Steve. You're not offering to just become my fitness coach. You're trying to change my whole life!" I said.

"You've got it," he said, "that's exactly right."

He was so disarmingly honest about it, "No, I'm not going to be your fitness coach, I'm going to change your life."

I said, "OK, sign me up."

After being his fitness student for a decade, at the age of fifty, Steve convinced me to try jiu-jitsu, a martial art taking place on the ground that focuses on techniques and maneuvers with the hands and feet that a smaller, weaker person can use to overtake a larger, stronger one. This is a sport where David can overtake Goliath using leverage and strategy, no slingshot required.

I began by reluctantly adding group classes in Brazilian jiu-jitsu to my regular fitness training.

Steve was right. I loved it instantly! Jiu-jitsu is strategy over strength, skill over size; it's three-dimensional chess.

This was a good fit for me, as I was never the athletic kid. I was always picked last for teams. Little League at the time was divided into major and minor leagues. I didn't even make it into the minor leagues. I was energetic and fit, certainly not a slob, but not well-coordinated and certainly not a fighter. So I was bullied, which ingrained in me the instinct, in confrontational situations, to back away and open the distance between the bully and myself. This is most people's natural response, open the distance, not close it.

But in some martial arts and fighting sports, closing the distance is the exact correct action. As in boxing, for instance, when the fighters are "in a clench" (which looks more like they're hugging), they can do almost no damage. They can't throw a punch and put their weight behind it because they're too close. In karate, if you're too close you can't successfully kick your opponent, you need a certain amount of space otherwise all you can do is step on his toes or kick him in the shins. So the natural tendency is to open the distance, to allow space to strike.

In jiu-jitsu, the most successful strategies involve doing the opposite of your instinctive reaction. Moving against your emotions is also what is required to be a successful investor. In jiu-jitsu, by grappling at extremely close range you reduce your opponent's capacity for punching and kicking while increasing your capacity for throws, joint locks, and chokes to bring them to submission.

Hold the opponent close with one hand...
Quick squat down with the other hand...
Heel pick...
Stand up quickly...
Step back with one hand still on his chest...
Push forward!
Opponent goes down.

It's inevitable. By virtue of the laws of physics, if he's on one leg, his torso is moving backward and his leg that you're holding is moving forward, he will fall onto his back. These are all things that I learned, and it made perfect sense to me. Jiu-jitsu went completely against "normal" thinking, which reinforced for me how success often requires overcoming your natural instincts, fears, reactions, and prejudices. It is overcoming your wrong common sense. It's about shifting out of autopilot into discomfort; settling there and being open to the possibility that the first action you feel like you should take might not be the right action. It might be correct, it might be wrong, just be open to the possibility either way. Shifting your narrative requires a willingness to be wrong.

There were about ten to twenty-five people in each class, mostly male, mostly in their twenties and thirties, and all sighted with full use of their bodies. Most had taken up the art as a form of self-defense. Despite my limitations (compared with those I grappled with), I became very good at jiu-jitsu. I was already fit and strong from a decade of training with Steve, and I have to confess, as an older "disabled" guy it was very satisfying beating up on those young kids. David versus Goliath.

More so than my eyesight, the bigger problem was my hands. I don't have any grip with my left hand and a very modest grip with my right. So I would fight on my back predominantly using my feet and legs. This strategy works well with jiu-jitsu since it's a non-striking martial art similar to judo or wrestling, no kicking or punching your opponent. Once again, Steve was right, it fit me perfectly.

The lesson here is also about playing your own game rather than trying to win at someone else's strategy, or succeed in someone else's narrative.

David changed the rules completely. He had no armor, nothing to limit his movement, and he fought from a great distance away from Goliath. The six-foot-seven giant used hand-to-hand combat, fighting up close to win his game. David never got in range and with his slingshot and pebble, essentially became the world's first sniper. Play your own game, no matter how big the competition is or how unlikely it seems that you will win.

Soon, after it was clear that I had gotten good at the sport, Steve had another big idea, that I should start competing. After winning several smaller, regional competitions I competed at the nationals in California, and won. My wife Natalia, a Brazilian jiu-jitsu competitor herself, Steve, and my other coaches encouraged me to go to the world championship held in Rio de Janeiro, Brazil.

Walking into the Brazilian arena was absolutely overwhelming. It was huge, confusing, and impossible to hear anything. The Seattle Seahawks NFL team calls their fans "the twelfth man on the field" because of the way their stadium is constructed to amplify noise. I was now to play my game in the middle of that chaos. Standing in the center of it all, I was scared to death and promptly made it to the restroom just in time to be sick.

They run six fights at the same time, resulting in the screaming echoes of fans cheering, coaches shouting, and bodies slapping onto plastic mats. Nobody can hear a thing, including the competitors. I was now fighting blind and deaf.

Nearing the end of my match, I was exhausted and on the brink of giving up. My arms and legs weighed a thousand pounds each and the noise had created a constant ringing in my ears. I became very disoriented, discouraged, and was seconds away from quitting. Then, through the din, I suddenly heard the voice of my Brazilian coach Solo Ravera, black belt, ten-time jiu-jitsu World Champion instructor. He was yelling something at me. I forced my mind to clear the ringing in my ears to make out what he was saying.

"No, don't give up Russell, if you could only see his face! You've got him! Push it!"

I don't know how, but I found some reserves, pushed through, got him in a chokehold and choked him out. Star Trek fans might recognize the result as similar to the "Vulcan Nerve Pinch" where the blood supply to the head is cut off by pressing critical blood vessels in the neck.

To my incredible surprise, I won the championship.

Solo later explained, "If you could see his face, you would see he was way more tired than you. He was only seconds away from tapping out. You had him."

Most people give up just when they're about to achieve success. They quit on the one-yard line. They give up at the last minute of the game one foot from a winning touchdown.
—Ross Perot

Then, I kept winning, outside the arena in Rio de Janeiro; I developed a following and became a minor local celebrity. Kids started following me around wherever I went. I didn't know what to make of this and was more amused than anything.

After winning that initial gold medal, to make sure it wasn't just luck, I went back and won two more golds in my weight division, along with two silvers and a bronze in the unlimited weight division where it truly was David versus Goliath. In all matches I fought sighted opponents.

Similar to wrestling, in jiu-jitsu you fight in your weight class, and that's where I was winning. In what would be my last competition I entered the unlimited weight division and fought against a really big guy, a true Goliath. When I entered the arena and walked onto the mat the crowd recognized me from prior years and I got an ovation. For once, I was not at all nervous and didn't get sick before the match. I had nothing to prove. I wasn't fighting for myself. My wife Natalia later said she could tell by my posture that I'd already decided I was going to lose. My declaration in that moment was not to win, but just to avoid getting hurt.

I did, however, make Goliath go the distance. I didn't submit and we went the full time of the match. He won on points, and received quiet applause for his victory. I earned a thundering standing ovation for not giving up. Although second place is where the losing starts, it won me a respect the goliath winner did not achieve.

POSTLUDE

In 2015 I gave a motivational talk at a local jiu-jitsu event here in Northern California. After the talk, one of the audience members came up and introduced himself as a jiu-jitsu coach named Henry. As it turns out, he was in Rio de Janeiro in 2005 and saw me in that last fight, when I won gold in my weight division but lost to Goliath in the unlimited weight division.

"You know Russell, whenever I think I'm up against something too hard in life, I think of you," he told me after my talk.

He added that whenever his students want to quit, he tells them my story. Then, he called over some of his students who were across the room to meet me.

"This is the guy I've been telling you all about," he told them. "This is the blind guy who won the gold and silver in Rio. This is him right here."

I felt humbled to play even a small role in inspiring others not to quit in the face of a challenge.

This role, of helping others lower the mental barriers of what they believe they can and cannot do, is one that has always come naturally to me. Naturally, however, doesn't always mean easily.

APRIL 2013

"What was I *thinking* when I said I would do this?" I thought, my mind racing with anxiety and thoughts of impending failure.

This could only end badly.

Standing in the stage wings in Bend, Oregon with my guide dog at my side, I was about to deliver a TEDx Talk to a largely entrepreneurially-minded audience of individuals looking to find inspiration and valuable messages from my life story. I thought they were crazy for even inviting me. This would be the first time I ever told my story publicly.

There had been a number of requests over the years, all of which I'd politely declined. This wasn't coming from a place of shyness, excessive humility, or any grandiose reason. I simply felt that the things that happened to me in my life were private, personal, not for public consumption, and honestly unremarkable.

TEDx Talks are strictly regulated for time and I was already having cold sweats about what would happen if I accidentally rambled for one second over the eighteen-minute time limit. Would there be a large hook to remove my guide dog and me from the stage?

With images of my large Mormon family and my hometown of Salt Lake City projected onto the screen behind me, I told my story—that of a mediocre high school boy who was no rocket scientist. But, inspired by President Kennedy's declaration that America would put a man on the moon and bring him back alive by the end of the decade, the boy managed to blow himself up while trying to build a rocket, losing eyesight first in one eye and then the other, and also mangling his hands. Then, pursuing a career in investing based on the declaration that he would not be poor and dependent on others, the boy went on to create a life narrative of his own choosing. He chose this versus taking on (what others saw as) the life of a "blind man." His career narrative would be one of a multi-millionaire investor, while his personal narrative would be one of defying expectations. At the age of fifty, for instance, egged on by his personal trainer, the man with no eyesight, no use of one hand, and very limited use of the other, decided to take on the martial art of jiu-jitsu. The opponents he faced were younger, sighted, and had use of all their appendages. Nevertheless, the man saw jiu-jitsu as a form of 3D chess and used his mind to adapt the physicality of the sport to his situation. He became adept at using his feet rather than his hands and fighting on his back for maximum control. Then, he became a three time Brazilian Jiu-Jitsu World Champion while fighting sighted opponents.

The journey that his life had become, as it turned out, was a story that people wanted to hear.

In addition to telling my personal story in that speech, I introduced an idea that has been a major grounding principle in my life, especially when defying expectations and charting my own course. The idea I presented was of making declarations of what you are *not* willing to tolerate (for me, being dependent on others), as a route to gaining what you want in life. I think most of those in the audience were used to hearing the reverse, the idea of creating a vision of what you *do* want and then going after it. There's nothing wrong with their way. I know it works for many people. I've just personally found that declaring what you will not tolerate has worked pretty well for me, dating all the way back to that day in the hospital after my final eye surgery.

At the TEDx Talk, I left it for each individual in the audience to decide what worked best for his or her life. And at the end of this book, when we part ways, I will leave you with that same choice. Whether you choose to shift or not shift your narrative is entirely up to you.

In spite of my apprehensions the talk was very well received. I think I even smiled, so they tell me. The audience gave me an extremely enthusiastic response, a standing ovation.

That's when the thoughts started formulating in my mind. What if beyond "amazing, wonderful, and fantastic," I could share my story even more in-depth? ***What if I was able to drill down to the core of my message that you could shift the narrative of your life by changing your declarations and taking the right actions?*** Was it possible that anything I had to say could "move the needle" in some way and create a shift in how people looked at the plotline of their lives? At the very least I wanted to pose the question—is the narrative of your life working? Is it producing the results you want? Leaving the event that day, having just rewritten a prior declaration that "my story is private and of no interest to anyone," the idea of this book was born, how I shifted my narrative and how others can do the same.

Now that you've seen how I've shifted the various narratives of my life (thus far), we move into the part where I "mentor" you, so to speak. You're about to delve below the surface of my story and learn the key elements of a narrative and how to distinguish which narratives are limiting you. From there, you will learn the actions needed to shift them. This is where my life has the potential to transform yours. This is where the inspiration ends and your work begins.

*Loss of vision did not deter
Russell's competitive nature.*

*Immersed in culture while visiting the home of a local
family that was inspired by Russell to start a school for
blind and disabled children in Jodpahur, India.*

Russell, competing in the BJJ Masters Seniors World Championship where he would earn three gold medals, two silvers and one bronze, fighting sighted opponents.

Competition Strategies in Jiu Jitsu: bait, hook, and remain one step ahead in the game.

The champion; standing high atop the medals platform at a Brazilian World Jiu-Jitsu Championship.

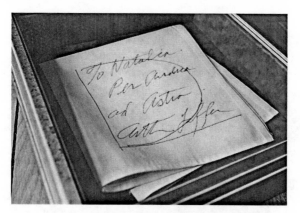

A napkin depicting the legendary Laffer Curve behind Latin meaning "From work to the stars." Written and signed by the famed economist and one of Russell's economic mentors Dr. Arthur Laffer. The original "Laffer Napkin," now housed in the Smithsonian, became a representation of the supply side notion that incentives alter behavior

Three generations of Redenbaughs. Russell riding his father's antique BMW with his son David.

Russell fishing and youngest son Jamie. Although he could not see the outdoors Russell instilled a love for it in his children.

Russell with granddaughter Isobel and guide dog Coulter.

From welfare to wealth; after being declared blind and "disabled" for life Russell Redenbaugh defied expectations, earning an MBA from Wharton, and then becoming Chief Investment Officer at a prominent Philadelphia money management firm that he helped grow to $6 billion in assets.

Russell's enjoyment outdoors leads him boating, camping, fishing and waterskiing.

Russell served as one of eight Commissioners on the U.S. Civil Rights Commission in Washington D.C. under three Presidents George, H. W. Bush, Bill Clinton and George W. Bush.

President George H.W. Bush in the White House Rose Garden at the announcement of Russell's appointment to the United States Commission on Civil Rights. His guide dog Royce is by his side.

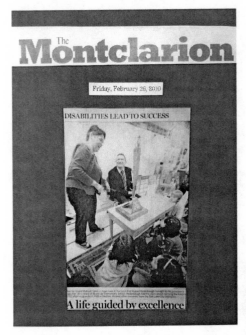

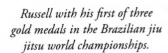

Russell doing show & tell at a local school where he told stories of being more in your life.

Russell with his first of three gold medals in the Brazilian jiu jitsu world championships.

Russell and his youngest son Jamie carrying the torch for the 2002 Winter Olympics held in Salt Lake City.

*Russell, daughter Allie, youngest son Jamie
and an event planner as part of the
2002 Winter Olympics.*

*Parasailing in Bermuda, where
Russell was attending an economic
summit on tax policy and incentives.*

*"Mood is everything and
narratives are the rest."
—Russell Redenbaugh*

In 2016, posing with tokens representing a lifetime of accomplishments.

Visiting Stone Henge in 2010, a site that resonates with Russell because of its permanent example of human achievement. We marvel at the declaration of Stone Henge without knowing the "How?" or "Why?"

Teaching the next generation to swim.

Below: Learning other cultures on a study tour of India.

Understanding foreign trade on the Silk Road.

Working with a child at the "Russell School" in northern India, a school for blind students inspired by Russell's story.

Russell, with wife Natalia, has come a long way from humble beginnings.

Finally she says, "Yes." Russell and Natalia get engaged in front of the world's most famous monument to love.

SECTION II
DRIFT

CHAPTER 6
WHAT YOU "KNOW"

Following the accident, my physical conditions resulted in an agonizingly long purgatory. The doctors (along with my nervous mother) were concerned that if I moved too much, the retina in my remaining eye would detach leaving me blind. As it turns out, their multiple eye surgeries to "fix it" inadvertently did this. Lying in limbo waiting to know if I would be living in the sighted world or darkness was more debilitating than being blind. The indecision and inability to plan and move forward was depressing.

The final news of my blindness forced me to choose between the disabling stories the doctors, my mother, and society shared or a heroic story filled with challenges and obstacles. That I was blind was out of my and the doctors' control, but I could choose how to deal with my circumstances. My father and I set about creating a story of challenge, yet success. It was the classic choice: see the glass as half empty or half full.

My father and I chose half full. Not because we believed this, but because the glass half full story opened rather than closed opportunities.

This choice, as difficult as it seemed, was still a relief. It was a choice, my choice. Before my accident, I had been living my life as a normal sighted teenager. I may not have been a role model, but I acted like a normal kid. My accident made returning to normal impossible. The challenges seemed insurmountable and could be ignored as long as the doctors continued pursuing surgeries in hope. But once it was clear nothing could be done to restore my sight, the die was cast and now I had to choose how to cope. My circumstances changed; I was now blind and would remain so. I would need to learn to see, act and be different in the world. I had a lot to learn.

My purgatory left me unable to act. Many of us have been paralyzed at one time or another unable to act. I've observed another more common purgatory with which most of us are familiar. This is the purgatory of indecision, conflict, and suffering. This can be caused by a self-limiting story. Many of us, consciously or unconsciously, live in a limiting "narrative." This is the DRIFT that goes unconscious or unresolved causing suffering. Now, I hope you don't feel singled out when I ask, is this you? Are you getting the results you want from your life? Is your narrative serving you?

NO QUICK FIXES

How is setting a new narrative course different than setting a goal, especially Stephen Covey's very popular S.M.A.R.T. (specific, measurable, actionable, results oriented, timely) goals? Well, a S.M.A.R.T. goal is actually a type of declaration (the starting point of a narrative). A declaration describes a specific goal, is measurable, and requires action in order for it to be successful. I have nothing against S.M.A.R.T. goals;

they're much better than stupid goals. Mr. Covey has helped far more people then I will ever reach. He has operationalized goal setting in a way that is implementable in life, and I admire his work tremendously.

S.M.A.R.T. goals work exceptionally well for highly motivated people who aren't impaired by disabling narratives. Take a moment to count how many people you know who aren't even somewhat impaired by a narrative that is keeping them from moving forward.

The fact is, when it comes to life improvement (or any type of) solutions, there are many roads to Rome. The limitation of S.M.A.R.T. goals and other "one and done" strategies is that they may not ultimately shift your life narrative.

However if S.M.A.R.T. goals, or other techniques are already working in your life, leading you to a narrative that works, you don't really need to keep reading this book. If everything is fine and working out, please find one of the many people for whom other systems of goal setting have *not* worked, and give them your copy. It certainly can't hurt to pay forward any solutions that make life work better, can it?

If you're still reading, then perhaps you are living in a narrative that's holding you back. Maybe, long ago, you accepted a declaration (or many) assigned to you by your family, your culture, your church, your country—or fill in the blank. And now those declarations have set the course to somewhere you didn't want to go. How would you feel about the opportunity to course-correct and create a narrative that takes you where you want to go?

My intention is simply to present you with the options—shift your narrative or don't. Some piece of the model I'm about to share with you, and the tools that go with it, will support a shift. In short, you may *choose* your life narrative instead of living the one that's been *adopted* by you.

All human beings live in narratives; this is how we communicate and relate to others. We grow up with different stories about the world and ourselves. Suffering happens when we live in a dissatisfying story. Sometimes we live in conflicting stories. Sometimes we live a story unrealized due to lack of action. Sometimes we act without connection to anything meaningful. All of this produces suffering and a mood. These moods are symptoms of missing actions or stories and signal where to further investigate.

Furthermore we reinforce narratives with the company we keep. Birds of a feather flock together. We not only tend to seek out people who are similar to ourselves, but the more time we spend *with* each other, the more similar we become *to* each other. People connect, relate and communicate through storytelling or narratives. Every day we share stories with others; we edit through selection or detail the stories we tell as our way to belong. "I'm a wine enthusiast" is something you might share with friends but not necessarily advertise with recovering alcoholics. Just as people try to match moods, they also choose and modify narratives to match the company they keep. In the interactions we have with one another we, in fact, modify one another. Clearly our narratives are based in language and as we interact with people our language and narrative can change. We all see this when a child has a new school friend and immediately adopts the new speech pattern, attitudes and values of the newfound companion. As Nietzsche wrote, "And if you gaze long into an abyss, the abyss also gazes into you." Your narrative grows because similar supporting narratives reinforce it.

Think of cable news! There is FOX, CNN, and MSNBC. Conservative Republicans watch FOX while Democrats watch MSNBC. Audiences seek out like-minded commentators for their news. Social networking is in part based on like-minded friends connecting; Facebook even has a "like" button on their site.

Are you living in an expired narrative? Are you mimicking actions of those whose success you admire, without a deep understanding behind those actions? A true shift cannot happen from the surface. A narrative shift comes from the core.

More than setting goals and hoping for change, shifting the entire narrative of your life means going very deep and swapping out all the things that are not working. We start with a declaration to end the conflict or suffering. This will change your mood. We then invent a narrative or story we try on, test, modify, and develop. Finally we move into action. If the whole car is broken, changing the oil isn't going to fix it. It's a holistic process, meaning that the "whole picture," the sum of all the parts, is looked at and changed. This is not the developmental equivalent of losing two pounds after the holidays. No, it is more likely a compounding result, possibly a lifetime of certain declarations you've made (consciously or subconsciously) and actions you've taken that have changed your original narrative.

Are you where you thought you'd end up? Or did something shift at some point and you can't really put your finger on what it was and when it happened? It was by complex change that you arrived here and that's what it will take to set a new course.

This thinking, of profound transformational change, is how, when I turned fifty, a friend named Steve Maxwell put me on the path of transformation from a blind investment advisor working at a desk with limited use of his hands, into a Brazilian jiu-jitsu black belt and three time world champion fighting sighted opponents.

Declarations are the first step toward shifting your narrative; they are the announcement of a new possibility. This is one reason why declarations are. Declarations open new possibilities and close others. Sometimes a declaration simply states what you *don't* want or will *not* do.

UNEXAMINED ASSUMPTIONS

There are, of course, so many other paths that my jiu-jitsu story could have taken based on various declarations hidden in my subconscious or accepted by others. What if I believed that a blind person couldn't do jiu-jitsu? Or I thought that I was too old to compete? Or perhaps I decided that my hands would prevent me from succeeding? Sometimes we put these declarations in our own heads, but more often than not, many beliefs have always existed. We've been walking through our lives with a certain set of unexamined assumptions about ourselves, others, and life in general, that limit us.

These assumptions could be false, but without close examination, how will you ever know? After a long enough period of time, they're taken as a given state of nature. In other words they become reality.

Have you heard, "they say" or "all the experts say"? Fill in the blank, whether it's about the hole in the ozone layer, things that will kill us from cancer, or that a diversified portfolio will protect your retirement assets. They say it, and without close examination of the facts, you believe it.

Money tends to be a magnet for unexamined assumptions. For some people, declarations about what they believe to be true about money and people who have it can be crippling. What if you held the unexamined assumption that money is bad, and therefore if you have money, you must have done something bad to get it? The idea that having money and being a humane, caring person cannot exist together seems to be common; the morality of poverty. People living with this declaration often believe their value is work done by the hour, versus their overall worth. Here is something to ponder—what if income was nothing more than a declaration? What if you were able to change the number, move the north star of your financial perceptions, by changing your language, and then making a declaration of what you will and will not tolerate about money?

My personal journey has been from welfare to wealth because for me, welfare was unacceptable. I also never thought of wealth as something evil, or as a value existing in contrast to being a virtuous person. If you live in a story, a narrative, where money is bad, you are unlikely to have a whole lot of it, because you are unlikely to take the actions needed to acquire it.

But even with these often-unexplored assumptions in place about money, the outcome of "being rich" is still a highly-coveted narrative. You turn on the television and watch *Entertainment Tonight* or another celebrity news show, you see the popular culture of flash, dash, and cash in story after story. It's exciting, sexy, and tantalizing; the expendable cash, red carpet, limousine lifestyle. Your imagination kicks in.

"Must be nice... I want that."

What is hidden, unseen on those shows is the amount of hard work, skill, and discipline it took to arrive on that red carpet. The money didn't just fall from the sky. It took certain declarations and actions to create that narrative. This also applies to any of the other executives, bankers, sports figures, entrepreneurs, anyone you look at and say...

"Must be nice... I want that."

It takes an incredibly strong person to stick to the declaration they've made about how much wealth they want to acquire and which actions they are willing to take, day after day, to acquire it. And if any of the declarations are contradictory—money is bad, people with money are bad, I don't deserve to keep it, etc.—there is a slim chance that the money will stay in their wallet. This is a pervasive narrative.

Do you know what every lottery winner learns right away? They learn that their family is much larger than they thought. Third cousins once removed come out of the woodwork, hand extended for their piece of the pie. For the lottery winner, the sudden outcome, without the steps it took to earn this windfall, is extremely disorienting. They are suddenly living in a dramatically different life narrative. As a result, many tend to "lose" their winnings and shift back to a more familiar, but limiting narrative: "We prefer a familiar swamp to an unknown Camelot."

SEEKING NARRATIVES

Erik Weihenmayer, the only blind person ever to climb Mt. Everest, made an interesting observation on his way up. He said that on the road to the peak of Everest you find many people who are more campers than climbers. They are dream tourists, making tracks through someone else's, but not really doing anything. They tell anyone who listens that they're going to be mountain climbers, but they're really just camping at the lower levels.

This happens in life off the mountain too. The billionaire investor Mark Cuban coined a term for people who aspire to become entrepreneurs but don't take the necessary actions, "wanna-preneurs." They know they don't want a "job" but they don't necessarily want to put in the work of building their own business from the ground up. They're camping on the lower levels of the mountain, hoping someone will come by and carry them up. They want the reward but without the work.

I'm sure if you survey any MBA class and ask, "Which of you want to be leaders?" every single hand will go up. Well of course I want to be a leader, because that's the right answer. That's what I'm supposed to want to be. So the automatic reaction is to raise their hands. Leaders have a profound responsibility to take care of the concerns of the company as well as the lives of the people they lead. It's not an easy job. But many of the MBA students chime in without even a shallow understanding. Just like the person who quits his job to become an entrepreneur without a full understanding of what's involved or the wannabe mountain climber without a plan to reach the top.

You need to understand the mechanics of the phenomenon that you wish to achieve. Henry Ford didn't try to biologically engineer a faster horse. Steve Jobs looked at technology that needed to happen, versus rewriting an old narrative that was already played out.

What story is trapping you? What story will free you to move forward? That is the story you need. That is your new narrative.

CHAPTER 7

DEFINING NARRATIVES

WHAT IS A NARRATIVE?

A narrative, quite simply, is the kind of story that explains one's events and experiences, whether true or not. Through storytelling human beings, are able to observe, communicate and relate using language. This is because we all live in language. Part of what makes us human is language. As babies, learning to speak is the first step in the journey from complete helplessness to independence. Language is what allows us to couple, operate, and coordinate with other human beings and create societies. Other animals may have communication, but our language allows us to build narratives rich with opinions and facts (assessments and assertions) propelled forward through interaction (promises, requests, offers, and commitments).

Narratives start with a declaration. President Kennedy made the powerful, big picture declaration that America would "put a man on the moon and bring him back alive in this decade." So what followed were all the conversations and actions needed to make that happen. Americans adopted a narrative about the US landing on the moon. Government launched conversations in science, finance, and policy. Narratives across the country changed as everyone saw space travel as a possibility. Americans were now part of the Space Race. Nationwide pride swelled as space travel became part of the American story.

To make Kennedy's declaration come to pass meant creating an organization called NASA, funding and staffing it, researching the science needed to make it all work and also, for at least ten years anyway, making the "space program" part of our national narrative. We were going to the moon and with each step covered by the media, from tragedies to triumphs, America cheered on the astronauts and scientists who were making it happen.

In fact, in the movie *The Right Stuff* based on Tom Wolfe's book, there's a scene that brings to life the importance of the national narrative and dreams ignited by Kennedy's declaration.

In the scene, the NASA scientists and test pilots, soon to be astronauts, are arguing about whether the hatch on the Mercury 7 space capsule needs explosive bolts so the astronauts can open the door themselves in case of an emergency. The scientists insist that this is the final version of the space capsule and no further changes will be made. The test pilots square up, look the scientists in the eyes and remind them what fuels the space narrative, and their jobs.

Pilot Gordon Cooper, played by Dennis Quaid, says to the scientists, "Do you boys know what makes this bird go up? Funding makes this bird go up."

Gus Grissom (via actor Fred Ward) backs him, saying, "That's right. No bucks… No Buck Rogers."

The others chime in and make their point. "Without the safety of explosive bolts, we're not going."

Narratives are the connective tissues of the events of our lives. They are the stories we tell ourselves. We use them to identify with whom we wish to connect, because the deepest human need is belonging.

EXAMPLES OF NARRATIVES

Parenting Success

Most have heard of Warren Buffett but not his older but junior partner Charlie Munger. Buffett is unlikely to leave a single dime of his billions to his two sons. Charlie Munger admits to being more patient than Warren. He said that if his heirs don't deserve the money, it will return to its rightful owners. If they don't know how to keep it, they won't.

I've seen this many times and there are many sayings around it like "shirtsleeves to shirtsleeves in three generations." Rarely do children outperform their parents, if the parents are top performers. Author Malcom Gladwell said in his book *Outliers* that the top performers on Wall Street and in law, tend to come from lower middle class backgrounds. The ones that come from upper class backgrounds tend to acquire bad habits because we, their parents, use our money to protect them from the consequences of their foolish actions. When we interrupt the process of learning, a sense of entitlement results. They can do no wrong and life can do no wrong to them. The authority to spend your parents' money without taking any responsibility for your life is a formula for failure.

Yet it is so tempting to try and protect our children from harm. Like so many others, I am guilty of this as a parent of three children, ranging in age from late twenties to early thirties. Jamie, my youngest, is named after the partner at Cooke & Bieler who hired me. Allie, my middle child, is adopted and most similar to me in personality and physically most like my wife, Natalia. David is my oldest, and named after my brother, whom you will learn about later in the book. David thinks most like me, but he has a better sense of humor!

I've learned over the years, and sometimes the hard way, that there are life experiences that you can't buy or bypass for your kids. They have to learn for themselves.

Some people call this "tough love." It's beyond that. Because by sheltering your kids from the world in a way that completely shields them from any sort of danger, you're failing to let them see how the world works. You're setting them up for failure by telling them what gifted geniuses they are; what special snowflakes they are to the world. Everyone wins. Everyone gets a prize. Those of us in the real world know that to be untrue.

Natalia's brother has three children and one time they came to stay with us at our home in Florida. One muggy Florida afternoon, Jared, the seven-year-old boy was guiding me to the bank and I spotted a teachable moment. I can't resist teaching, especially when it comes to money matters.

"Jared," I asked him as we navigated down the bustling town street, "Where does money come from?"

"My mom and dad," he answered in kind of a "duh!" tone.

"Yes, but where do they get it?" I asked.

"Well, they go to work," he answered.

"Oh, so they do a job?" I asked.

"I guess," the boy responded.

"And how do banks make money?" I asked as we entered the chilly air-conditioned bank lobby from the furnace outside.

"They hold your money," Jared said.

"Yes, that's what they do, but how do they MAKE money?" I pressed.

"Well," he said, "I'm not sure but they must do some job."

That's when the idea of the "job jar" was born. To teach and reinforce to the kids that money comes from doing jobs, Natalia and I took an empty peanut butter jar and wrote the names of little jobs and what each job paid on scraps of paper and put them in the jar; folding laundry, washing dishes, polishing furniture, picking up dog poop, and such. When any of the three kids wanted money, we told them to reach into the job jar and fish out a job. So, when a kid came and begged for money for candy or comic books, we said, "No, because how does money happen?" and the kid would remember, "Ohhhh, the job jar," and scurry off to select a job to do. From then on, whenever the kids would visit, Natalia and I would pull out the job jar and put everyone to work to exchange money for jobs. Later on, Jared and his brother, Alex made $200 one winter shoveling snow in Boston, which was a lot of money for kids their age.

We also took the kids to a kids' resort called Wannado City, where only Wannado City money was accepted; nothing from the U.S. Mint. But in order to spend the Wannado money, first you need to earn it. Similar to the job jar, kids can pick the jobs they want to do. Jared's brother, Alex, and baby sister, Lydia chose to be firemen so they gave them little fireman suits, trained them about the job, and gave them a fake fire to put out to earn the money needed to buy a slice of pizza for lunch. Of course, my wife Natalia raced behind capturing the moment on her camera with our sister-in-law.

All three kids learned from the job jar and Wannado City that money is earned from doing a job, not from asking for it from Mom, Dad, Uncle Russell, Aunt Natalia, the bank, or an ATM machine. I think there's a certain percentage of the population today who could benefit from a trip to Wannado City.

Rather than simply doling out "money lessons" as many parents tend to do, the stronger choice would be to help children consciously build an actionable, financial narrative that brings the information to life versus just preaching dos and don'ts of money. Invent games similar to the job jar! Make learning and shifting narratives fun and meaningful!

Unfortunately I learned this lesson too late for my children but I'm passing it on.

Unicorns

The investment and economics industries are filled with narratives, many of which are deeply flawed. Some of these deeply held investing narratives are no longer true today, if they were ever true. I, along with my friend and business partner James Juliano, have built an investment advisory business (Kairos Capital Advisors) and an investment research business (Policy Based Investing) to reveal these broken investment narratives and put people on better paths to protect and grow their wealth.

One common Wall Street narrative is being a "true believer" seeking unicorns and Cinderella. Many investment professionals try finding companies that appear to be scullery maids but are really princesses. Naturally, Wall Street "true believers" find more Cinderella stocks than exist. Their narrative about finding the next IPO soon-to-be Apple or Google guides their investment actions, often to the detriment of their clients' wealth.

Another wrong Wall Street narrative is that diversification will protect you. The theory is that since different assets are uncorrelated, owning some of everything can offset risks. But when a crisis happens there is, in effect, a giant margin call on all assets. Negative correlations between different assets become positive as all are offered for cash. As my business partner James wrote in a recent "Policy Based Investing" report, "The last three years, like numerous multi-year periods throughout history, are a clear example that diversification is a 'fool's game' in that it allows one to reach mediocre results from whichever side one starts. We do not believe in diversified portfolios. Contrary to conventional wisdom, diversification is what you do when you don't know what to do."

Another wrong investing narrative is that as you age you should own more bonds to reduce portfolio risk. This used to work just fine when bond rates were high, but now with bond interest rates artificially suppressed by the government, AAA and government bonds may decline thirty to fifty percent when interest rates normalize higher. These are not the low risk assets one near retirement should be investing in.

James' and my entire role as investment advisory partners is to reveal how these dangerous narratives harm wealth. We help clients find more powerful narratives to protect and grow their capital. We believe that our narrative called "Policy Based Investing," where asset prices are determined by government economic policies, is a more powerful and lucrative story to invest within as opposed to commonly "sold" Wall Street myths that have failed time and again.

To learn more about more dangerous narratives that impact investors you can download our free ebook at KairosCapitalAdvisors.com: *Top 3 Mistakes Investors Make: A High Net Worth Investor's Guide on How to Avoid Them.*

CHAPTER 8
THE STORY THAT FREES YOU

Full disclosure—change is hard. As my wife Natalia learned from years as an international business consultant for corporations like IBM, Applied Materials, and KLA Tencor, there is a 10-10 Rule: unless there's a ten times return, you're not going to get people to change more than ten percent.

We also know this from Nobel Prize winning behavioral economist Daniel Kahneman's work. A loss is twice as painful as an equivalent size gain. People avoid losses with twice the aversion that they pursue gains in a risk-based situation. Now this could just be some leftover evolutionary DNA lingering from when our ancestors had to outrun tigers in order to survive, but it limits our willingness to take risks today. In simplest modern terms, Kahneman's theories are the reason why most New Year's fitness resolutions fail and gyms that are packed in January and February, are ghost towns by spring. The benefit is not at least twice as appealing as the pain and inconvenience.

I continue to look on with amusement (and a slight amount of pity) at the people who are on a lifelong search for the holy grail of self-improvement, the completely painless, risk-free, transformational "life change" pill. There is no return without risk and effort. Trust me, I've studied the idea of "return" from every possible angle throughout my career as an investment professional, and there's no way around it.

Ignore and avoid the victims, the magic pill seekers, or anyone else you know with a disabling narrative that is not serving his or her life. This book is about the possibilities for *your* life. You have come to the proverbial fork in the road. One path appears to be risk free, painless, and has a small return on investment, but possibly one you can live with, because you've lived with it just fine up until now. Or you can venture down the other path, one of change and transformation. I am presenting you with the opportunity to change the declarations that have defined your life until this point, and take the actions necessary to free yourself from a narrative that is not serving you, and create one that will. You are in charge here.

REWRITING THE STORY

When and why do we rewrite stories? When the narrative, its style, values, and actions don't match ours OR when there is a conflict between the stories and/or actions we are living in.

The actual rewrite however, takes courage. In the Oscar award-winning film *Good Will Hunting*, the character Will, played by Matt Damon, lives an honorable, working-class narrative in blue-collar South Boston, largely powered by the people he surrounds himself with. As his psychologist notes (played by the late, great Robin Williams), "Those guys would lay down in traffic for you." The people you surround yourself with (friends, colleagues, spouse) can influence the story you tell yourself. But from the opening scene of the film, we see that Will doesn't fit in with his working-class friends as much as he might like to think. For years he has been studying and training his brain and he is without doubt a mathematical genius. It is impossible for this life narrative to stay bottled up forever and, inevitably, word of his genius leaks out, and makes its way up the hierarchy of Harvard mathematicians. Soon the government pursues his employment to solve some of its most complicated math problems. Will very colorfully tells the men in suits where to go and returns to his job at a construction site. The clash between narratives, working-class versus Ivy League, is too much to integrate. Will feels safer and more comfortable with his buddies in their working-class narrative. The Boston-based working-class lifestyle with his neighborhood buddies is the only life story he has ever known. Through a series of events, realizations, and conversations with his psychologist, Will eventually sees that there is a whole other life available to him and he drives off into the horizon. Most people don't have a friend, played by Ben Affleck, with the character to encourage them to make such a life-changing shift.

SHIFTING NARRATIVES

It was 1988, South Korea was hosting the Olympic Games. Back here in the States, the photo giant, Kodak, was in its prime, employing 145,000 people. The company's success was largely due to public demand for photographic film and paper (remember that stuff you had to get developed before digital cameras were invented?).

I was on an airplane, where I practically lived in those days, commuting back and forth between Philadelphia and Silicon Valley. On this particular flight I was sitting in first class next to a man who was on his way to the Olympics in South Korea. He worked for Eastman Kodak. At the time they were seeing nearly seventy percent gross margins in film sales. But digital photography was on the horizon. Working in technology, I saw how quickly digital was catching on, and I was of course eager to get his point of view. Especially, as I found out, since he worked in the emerging digital division of Kodak.

"What are your plans for digital photography?" I asked him.

"We're really not focusing much on digital," he admitted. "We don't see it as an alternative to film at all. The quality is so terrible I think it's a non-issue."

"Well, how many Moore's Laws doubling cycles will it take until the quality is good enough to take over a big part of your market?" I asked him.

Moore's Law[1] refers to an observation made in 1965 by Gordon Moore, the co-founder of Intel. He observed that the number of transistors per square inch on integrated circuits had doubled every eighteen months since the integrated circuit was invented. He then predicted that the trend would continue.

This had not occurred to my seatmate, the Kodak executive from the digital division.

"Well, I never even thought about it that way," he said, and paused before continuing, "But I still don't think it [digital] is going to be a problem for us because the quality isn't there."

He was right—at the time

Digital filmmaking was just entering the experimental stages, and by 1999 George Lucas changed the film landscape by shooting *Star Wars Episode I: The Phantom Menace* entirely on digital. But for the time being, my seatmate was correct about digital photography, the quality wasn't there but he had much to worry about.

Unfortunately for Kodak, Moore's Law of doubling continued on schedule, and the quality of digital photography multiplied dramatically. Kodak didn't see it coming, or in my seatmate's words, "didn't see it as a big problem." They were taking actions based on the useless, though

1   http://www.webopedia.com/TERM/M/Moores_Law.html

accurate, assumption that the quality of digital film was poor and would not improve soon. There was another thing that Kodak failed to take into consideration that contributed to these blind spots. They were so busy looking at the high-end photography/art market that they failed to see the biggest portion of their market, family photos developed at Kodak photo kiosks. For families, even "less than perfect" digital quality would be acceptable. Especially, if it meant getting adorable photos of their kids developed even faster to show off in the family photo album or email instantly to grandparents. Kodak was so embedded inside their own traditions that they were blind to how the game was not only changing, but would continue to change at an accelerating rate.

The company started losing power long before they realized it and long before it showed up in any of their financials. They ultimately ignored the threat on the horizon.

Kodak's inability to speculate about the future cost them the company. In 2012 they filed for Chapter 11 bankruptcy protection and then announced the end of production of digital cameras and similar products. By the end of that year they sold every division except motion picture film, still fighting to get out of bankruptcy. In 2013 Kodak sold many of its patents to companies including Apple, Google, Facebook, Amazon, and Microsoft.

Another example of costly corporate blindness is Sean Fanning and Napster, starting an online music revolution. However, since the core mechanism of the revolution was illegal piracy, it only got so far before the music industry decided to start suing teenage boys for downloading music from each other's hard drives. This did not seem like a winning strategy from the vantage point of cash awards or from being able to stop what soon became rampant downloading of music, more than any authorities could possibly have controlled.

The question that emerged for the music industry was: how are we going to prevent the unpreventable? Then along came Steve Jobs, who understood intellectual property because of Pixar, in addition to his little computer hardware and software company called Apple. Jobs won the trust of the music industry and set up iTunes, pointing out (paraphrasing his intended message), "Look you're not going to make as much money, but the way you're doing it now, the record stores are going to go broke. You need to get with the program or you too will go out of business."

He went on to promise to keep the integrity of the transactions intact and copyright the product. This was clearly the best deal the music industry was going to get, unless they wanted to devote their profits into creating a full-time security force to go around arresting college students every time they downloaded a song in their dorm rooms. Times had changed, and the way that things were being produced had also changed. Bending plastic into a CD, shipping it, and stocking it in stores had turned a very costly process versus downloading the production bits, not atoms.

The writing was on the wall, physical "recording" was becoming a costly dinosaur that nobody wanted to house anymore. Unlike Kodak, the record companies and artists knew that different actions were needed to survive. Steve Jobs, in a way, forced the music industry to adapt to new conditions and to their credit, they took the deal and today people go to places like iTunes for their music.

The wrong narrative can have serious and often dire consequences. In business, it can be deadly. For Kodak, this failure to shift cost all the employees their jobs and all the shareholders their wealth. Unfortunately examples like these have continued, year after year. Blockbuster, for example, failed because they were in denial about the cost of bandwidth, which had always been a very scarce resource. They assumed bandwidth would continue to be scarce. They missed what George Gilder in his book *Telecosm* described as the thousand fold cost cliff that bandwidth would soon fall down. I mentioned at the top of the book, the hidden costs of not shifting your personal narrative. At the corporate level, you're not just costing yourself but now you're affecting other people's lives.

There are many companies and industries that have missed the narrative shift from moving atoms to moving bits. There is no more distance in long distance.

IMAGINE A NEW NARRATIVE

In the Stephen King novel, *Duma Key*, main character Edgar Freemantle said, "God punishes us for that which we cannot imagine." Every narrative shift begins as an idea.

Fiction authors and screenwriters have a process for determining a moral and behavioral foundation of their characters. Let's make up a character named Bob and say that he is the main character in a romantic comedy about getting the girl of his dreams. When developing Bob's character, the writer will establish things that the character is and is not, and what the person would and would not do. It has already been ruled out, what Bob would and wouldn't do in any given circumstance. The character Bob has established a declaration in his story: get the girl. His narrative is the story of what he will and will not do, and how he will live his life on the journey of getting the girl.

Living your narrative means understanding which actions are consistent (and not consistent) with your structure and make-up as a person. Once you understand this, you can anticipate how you will handle various situations, rather than stopping each time and making a decision.

You are probably doing this all the time without even realizing it. For the vast majority of people, it's very difficult to take actions that are inconsistent with their narrative. Do you know the narrative from which you are working? When you take an action, do you always know why? Bob does because the screenwriter dictates his actions. But who's dictating yours?

If you can't first imagine something, perhaps it's because nobody ever brought it up to you as a possibility. If you're poor and everybody you know is poor, then there is no new movie plotline to go after. If you can't imagine being anything other than poor, it's highly likely that you will stay poor. Shifting your narrative means writing a new story of what can and cannot exist. You can be the author of your narrative.

In contrast, what if you could somehow imagine that through some set of actions you could move away from being poor? This would open up a new set of possibilities to take those actions and produce results. As real-life characters, we move through the world imagining future action, and either shifting our narratives to align with them or carrying on as usual. The bottom line is, if you can't first imagine something as a possibility for your life then it's unlikely it will ever happen. Imagining is not nearly enough.

BEING MORE

I met Charles at our "Max-ercise" personal training sessions twenty years ago, around the time I got into jiu-jitsu. He was working as a field technician for IBM. In talking with Charles, it became rather obvious to me that the view he had of possibilities for his career and his life was pretty limited. He was obviously a very intelligent, capable, skilled guy with an engineering degree; but his narrative seemed to be "this is it for me." He had a visible lack of enthusiasm for what he considered to be a dead-end job. Of course he didn't come out and explicitly say these things, but the message that I heard by listening between the lines was clear. This is something I do quite a bit, by the way, listen between the lines—for me, a different kind of "seeing."

After jiu-jitsu one night, he came back to our house to visit and, over the kitchen table, I started talking to him about ambition.

"Ambition?" Charles asked, sounding confused.

"Yes, ambition. Here's the deal Charles, I'm blind, you're black. It is what it is. But WE CAN ALWAYS BE MORE."

We kept talking about how to build this idea of ambition and "being more" into building a new narrative for his life. I told him that, "All stories may be equally valid, but not all stories are equally powerful." This inspired Charles to craft a more powerful life story for himself. He began to build a new narrative where he would be a lifetime learner, open to seeing and creating new possibilities. He took ownership of where he was in life without blaming anyone else, and then put a plan in action to create a new narrative of "being more."

The actions that Charles took centered on two areas. First, linguistic awareness, which as I told him, means differentiating between assessments and assertions. There is no such thing as should or shouldn't, or right or wrong. There are only assessments and interpretations of those assessments. The second action that Charles took was listening for requests and identifying where to make offers (more powerful than requests since no organization survives if its offers are not accepted) and how to make and hold promises.

He also picked up quickly on my assertion that there are no problems; really, there is only what happened, what's missing, and what the next action is. Another one of those actions was to take business education courses to expand possible career options.

Charles emailed me recently, sharing how his life has changed.

"Russell, you killed the victim mindset in me. Today, it is supremely satisfying to live out of this new narrative of "being more"—my new life story. The declarations, narratives, and actions that you taught me, Russell, have given me a competitive advantage that helped me move from field technician into a successful management career and finally into a sales role at IBM."

He changed his narrative and then put himself into different actions.

Charles is not unique or unusual in his capacity to shift his narrative and change his life. Nor am I. Most people view my story from blind and on welfare to a myriad of successes as something remarkable, even unreal. This is not true. I was ordinary. I changed. You can too. In the final section of this book we move out of the theories about narratives into the action of shifting.

SECTION III
SHIFT

Your beliefs become your thoughts, Your thoughts become your words, Your words become your actions, Your actions become your habits, Your habits become your values, Your values become your destiny.

—Mahatma Gandhi

CHAPTER 9
MOODS

Mood is everything and narratives are the rest.
—Russell Redenbaugh

A couple hundred adult students sat in a West Coast auditorium waiting to hear me speak about how moods can shift your narrative, either for better or for worse. My assistant and I even had the clever idea of making three-inch buttons for the students that said one of my most used "Russell-isms," "Mood is everything and narratives are the rest." The students were eager to hear my words of wisdom on how to improve their mood, move into productive action, and shift their narrative for the better. The problem was, standing there backstage; I was in a really bad mood. Only thirty minutes before, I was back in my hotel room on a very unpleasant phone call with my wife.

We were in the process of divorcing, which understandably put me in a bad mood. Despite my assistant's best efforts to cheer me up, even going so far as to slap me across the face, I wasn't at all interested in talking to this audience, with their big "mood" buttons, about how to be in a good mood. Even as my guide dog started leading me out, I had no idea what I would tell them. I stepped into the center of the stage and adjusted my lapel mic.

"Mood is everything," I started, "and I am in a terrible mood right now. I just got off the phone with my wife. She and I are in the middle of a very unpleasant divorce."

That got a laugh. I was encouraged.

"Oh, I see some of you have been divorced and others of you are thinking about it," I said.

That got an even bigger laugh. My mood began to improve. Learning can only happen in certain moods, and laughter is one of them. My students (and I) were now ready to learn.

ON DEFEAT

Success takes a decade, failure can happen sooner.
—Russell Redenbaugh

There are no lessons in victories. A defeat, however, contains many.

I'm a person who hates to lose—it's almost unbearable to me. But the reality of life, as we all know, is that defeat happens.

What do you do when there is such a defeat? How do you keep your narrative on track and keep plugging forward? It would be wrong for me to say: oh, just shift your narrative, suck it up and move on. Failure can be a devastating blow. But in order to win, you must be able to handle the defeats, the losses, the depression, despair, and heartbreaks.

I don't always win; no one does. At times I am crushed and need to slowly recover my mood. It's not always easy to bounce back. Just like anyone else, I too am guilty of failing to shift my narrative, slumping down, and giving in to failure. One of the things that still, after all these years, I'm learning is how to pick my battles. Actually, I'm still learning every single thing that I'm writing about in this book. We are learning together.

You teach that which you most need to learn.
—Russell Redenbaugh

ACTIONABLE MOODS

Moving from inaction to action always improves your mood. In fact, I believe the entire spectrum of moods is actually derived from either being in action or not in action. Action is causal. The paralysis of indecision can produce a disabling, bad mood.

There are some actions that simply cannot happen if you're possessed by certain moods. An irritable, depressed, or angry mood, for instance, rarely leads to productive action. This can tunnel all the way down to despair, where the desperation can actually cycle you into action from sheer unwillingness to suffer for a moment longer.

Think of a mood as a conversation. A depressed mood is a conversation based around the notion that "life is messed up and everywhere I look I find the evidence to prove that, therefore there's no point in doing anything so I might as well just go back to bed."

The good news is, changing the conversation and shifting moods is a relatively straightforward process, once the awareness is there that your current mood is not productive. This is the key lesson. Identifying your moods is where the diagnosis begins. Follow the suffering.

I often use "mood reset" when this is the case. If the mood in a meeting is "off" for whatever reason, I bring an abrupt halt to things and then take specific actions to reset the mood in the room. I realize that if the meeting continues as is, nothing will really be accomplished except a roadblock of disagreement, so what is the point of moving on? Sometimes the resets involve playing certain music (appropriate to the age and group of people in the room), and others will be simply shifting the language of the conversation. Successful motivational speakers like Tony Robbins and television evangelists are masters at this.

In brainstorming conversations among a small group, you need a mood of speculation to avoid immediately killing off any ideas that could later blossom into something useful. A speculative, open mood in a brainstorming session leads to the action of putting everyone's ideas up on the whiteboard, without judgment or criticism. Even the blatantly bad ideas have the potential of triggering good ones.

My friend and colleague Drew Lebby was brought in to change the cultures of companies. He was a "company doctor," in a sense, which is a very hard thing be, especially when dealing with the "we've always done it this way" variety of long-standing, traditional corporations. By the way, the correct response to "We've always done it this way" is "Well, unfortunately the rest of the world doesn't care that you think that. Your competition in particular will actually be delighted that you continue to do what doesn't work."

One time I brought Drew into a company that I was consulting, a family-owned entity with third generation owners who defended their decisions mostly by repeating, "It worked this way for my grandfather."

We gathered the top executives, about seven of them in the conference room and my friend covered all the walls with butcher paper. He then handed the executives markers and had each one write out the company history from their perspective. Then they all walked around the room and came to an agreement on one overall story of the company history.

After that, Drew posed the question over and over, for each key piece of the history, "What were the circumstances that made that the right action at the time?"

What he was doing, was shifting the mindset from "we can't change because we haven't" to a mood of speculation, to think about the future instead. The group finally realized, as a result of this openness, that things are really quite different now than they were fifty years ago so perhaps they should take different actions.

In addition to problem solving, the action of learning, particularly in the mentorship experience, requires a specific mood, one of openness to admitting that you don't know what you don't know. This is especially true if what you're being told is contrary to your experience. To push through and see results, there has to be a mood of openness, of willingness to speculate and to trust the teacher.

There must be the open mindedness to say, "I don't agree with you but I know you wouldn't deceive me. Tell me more. That's very different from my experience. Why do you say that?"

NARRATIVES AND MOODS

Narratives can also shape moods. The Oxford dictionary defines mood as a temporary state of mind or feeling. I would add that a narrative accompanies this state of mind or feeling. Moods and narratives are tightly interconnected. An improved mood can open possibilities for new actions. Other moods can freeze you. It is important to be the observer of the question: In what mood do I find myself?

Moods distort the world you see.

We see the world, not as it is, but as we are—or as we are conditioned to see it.

—Stephen R. Covey

Certain narratives are associated with specific moods. Anxiety, for example, arises when there is a mismatch between narrative, action and meaning. Depression almost guarantees inaction. On the other hand, despair can compel action where depression smothers it.

Moods that reveal suffering are an excellent diagnostic tool. They tell the listener where to look. That is, which narratives or missing actions are producing the suffering. One of three things will be revealed: 1) inaction, 2) conflicting or incompatible narratives, or 3) a missing narrative.

Moods at both extremes, positive and negative, clearly cloud judgment. As we said before, observe your mood. It will distort your assumptions and could prejudice your actions. For example, a positive or "ecstatic mood" is not the right mood to be making investment decisions, nor is a negative or "panic" mood. It is important to manage mood when shifting narratives or enrolling others in your narrative. Moods can engage participation.

Moods and music are closely connected. Music can reflect the mood of the time. Music can also be used to shift moods and evoke story. Mozart produces a far different mood than Beethoven. Bob Dylan evokes a very different mood than Motown. The Rolling Stones could not be confused with the Beatles. The music of the 60s certainly evoked a very different mood than that of the 70s and 80s.

EASY RIDER

There is something I haven't told you about another reason that I made one of the biggest narrative shifts of my life, leaving Cooke & Bieler for Silicon Valley. It is also one of the most powerful lessons I've gained about mood shifts. It is the story of my brother David, who died at the age of thirty. I still miss him to this day, more than I sometimes admit.

David and the rest of the family called me "Zuz" growing up because I could not say Russell. My brother was twenty-one months younger, which created a fair amount of sibling rivalry. The whole setup seemed unfair to me at times. There would be certain privileges I couldn't get until a certain age, like a later bedtime, but then as soon as I got them he did too. He seemed to earn benefits by proxy rather than waiting.

But the accident that changed my life also changed everything between David and me. The rivalry disappeared and he became very supportive, taking care of me and assisting me in any ways he could. We became very close after that, doing things together socially like double dating, rock climbing, and riding in his airplane. In addition to flying planes, David also rode motorcycles, generally wore cowboy hats and boots, and enjoyed the wide-open spaces of the west; he was a free spirit in every sense of the word.

David's narrative was to stay independent no matter what, and always do his own thing. After a short stint in the Utah Air National Guard, he wanted to study aviation. But going to school interfered with his flying so he dropped out and started a skydiving school instead.

David's love of flying extended beyond piloting small planes and parachuting out of them, he was also into base-jumping. Base-jumping has a person wearing a nylon-flying suit with fabric winglets under their arms that expand when they jump, essentially turning them into a flying squirrel. Daredevils like David jump from high-rise buildings and bridges, where it's a straight, flat drop to the ground. They get a running start, bolt for the edge and dive.

This time, however, David had flown to California with some of his students to do an illegal base jump off El Capitan, one of the largest rocks at Yosemite National Park. It was the early 80s and he had just turned thirty. The reason this was a bad idea from the start, was because of the uneven shape of the rock. He and his friends needed to get an even more massive running start to get the momentum they needed to clear the cliff face, which sloped outward. They wouldn't be able to open their chutes until they cleared the rocky cliff. One by one, David's students ran, leapt, and cleared El Capitan. Then it was his turn. Taking a deep breath, David went into a full sprint, arms pumping, the thick textured rubber soles of his jump boots slapping against the rock. He jumped.

He may have leapt too soon and was too close to the cliff face. Instead of landing in the drop zone David fell with a loud, sickening thud onto some boulders in a nylon tangle of squirrel suit and parachute. He wasn't able to execute a PLF, parachute-landing fall, and ended up breaking one leg very seriously. He was airlifted out.

His leg was so severely broken that it ended up being an inch shorter than his uninjured leg. For an independent, physical guy, always on the move, this was a defeating blow. For the time being, Easy Rider was sidelined. He began the long arduous road of physical rehabilitation and threw himself into the task the best he could.

A couple other things also happened during the year preceding David's death. One night, while driving home, David steered his car into a blind curve on the highway. The US Army Guard truck broken down on the side of the road hadn't set out flares so David plowed right into it, creating a green metal mess. He wasn't hurt, but his car was totaled.

He loved that car, but he loved the girl he was living with at the time even more. When he learned she was unfaithful to him, he was crushed. This was a turning point from which David was never able to recover. That same night he found out, after what I can imagine was a fiery, emotional nightlong confrontation, David began drinking heavily and then added a sleeping pill to the mix.

I was in Dallas at the time, on a research trip for Cooke & Bieler. At roughly five o'clock in the morning, the bedside phone rang. It was another partner, my friend and former Wharton classmate Robert who'd gotten me my initial interview at Cooke & Bieler. Bob, with his Southern manners, grace, and refinement delivered the news. I could tell he was trying to be as gentle as possible.

July 19, 1981. David was dead of an accidental overdose.

My closest friend was dead. Despite David's known dark side, I can honestly say I did not see this coming, not in the least. David's unexpected death was, at the time, a bigger disaster than my own blindness. I had time to adjust to my own injuries and the overwhelming feeling was of relief that I finally got to move forward. His loss came all at once and I couldn't find a silver lining.

My brain worked overtime mulling over the details, trying to make sense of it. He was finally turning a corner in recovering from his base-jumping accident, and getting very physically fit. The word "accidental" seared itself into my brain. He was upset with his girlfriend, drank too much, and then added the sleeping pill and everything merged into a perfect storm, a tragedy. The coroner used the same word.

Accidental suicide.

This, of course, was purely a legal distinction. How do you accidentally kill yourself? Suicide without intent?

When we are no longer able to change a situation, we are challenged to change ourselves.
— **Viktor E. Frankl**, *Man's Search for Meaning*

You can't control what happens to you, but you can control how you feel about it and what you say about it, to yourself and others. You can find meaning in adverse circumstances, and you can choose your narrative to lead you out of those circumstances.

Accidental suicide…

This shifted my entire grieving process around David's death. The truth was, that it was an accidental suicide. He had undertaken the actions that accidentally led to his own death. This was not some terrible, unexplainable phenomenon that "happened" to David, or even me, or our family. It was true that it happened and now what was I going to say about it to myself? Was I going to be damaged, limited and restrained in my life narrative because these bad things "happened" to me, first my accident and then David's? Or, was I going to take responsibility for both things, from the standpoint of being the owner of everything that happens to me? There was no one to be angry at, to lash out at; it was exactly what it was. While others in my family kept a safe distance from their pain by stating, with forced certainty that David's death was "God's plan," the standpoint I was working from was one of personal ownership.

After David's death, I felt pushed to answer some of life's deeper philosophical and spiritual questions, ones that I'd never confronted before, even after my own accident. I needed to go to a place that was conducive to such an exploration.

The Esalen Institute in Big Sur on the Northern California coast, a spa with a hot water spring, has been around since the 1930s. Esalen was a magnet for some of the most famous philosophical and spiritual journeys because it was a very permissive place with few rules beyond "don't hurt each other."

Esalen was really what you want and need it to be for you. I went to Esalen almost immediately after David's death. His death was the push for me to answer some of the deeper philosophical and spiritual questions that had bubbled to the surface. Esalen was a place conducive to finding answers.

I met Will Schutz there, the Harvard professor and author who taught me that life will be better once you assume that you cause everything that happens to you. It doesn't happen because you're a bad person, or that you're being tested or prepared for something bigger. Is the "God's plan" theory really a shield to avoid confronting the fact that the universe is indifferent and random? The realization that the universe is abundant and probably random could create a very lonely existence. To think that life arose on Earth randomly is not the most comforting point of view. These are the types of life questions I grappled with while going on long hikes and soaking in the hot springs, pondering the words now etched deeply in my mind "accidental suicide."

The word "accidental" inevitably sent me backwards in my narrative to my own accident. I finally realized that I'd never really reconciled that life-changing event. Instead, from the moment I dictated the letter to the guide dog school, I became a laser-guided missile, locked on various targets based on my declarations, focused only on getting the job at hand done. Suddenly, I was confronting not only my brother's death, but also my own close call with it. Was this by design, random, or something I caused? My lack of chemistry skill had certainly caused the accident but was I also responsible for the severity of my injuries? In grieving my brother's death, I also began to grieve, for the very first time, the life that might have been for me.

A friend introduced me to the work of psychologist Elizabeth Kubler-Ross. She is well known for identifying the stages of grieving: denial, anger, bargaining, depression, and acceptance. I realized that, two decades after my accident, I was still in denial that it happened, or how I really felt about it. I read voraciously, searching every book for more answers and finding even more questions in the process. Jude Wanniski, famous political economist, talks about the contingency of life and how "change only happens on the margin." So when we look back, it's easier to see how it is those changes, that may have seemed minor at the time, led us down a very different path than the one we were on. These are things we rarely realize at the time.

Through these mental expeditions, I realized that the answers I had to the questions I was now confronting were not good enough. My existing answers were producing only misery and suffering. I even contemplated moving to Hong Kong just because it was a different part of the world. There were also parts of the world that I considered, where someone could disappear, live inexpensively, and not be found. But then I realized once I got there I would still be me. I couldn't disappear from myself.

This was around the same time that I felt suffocated at Cooke & Bieler, a racehorse in a traffic jam. David's death was a catalyst in my action to break free and head to Silicon Valley. I realized that more money would not produce more satisfaction or happiness. That hadn't worked so far; it just produced more money. David's passing created the spark that reminded me how important it is to live rather than to merely exist in a moldy narrative. So, I shifted my narrative.

CHAPTER 10
DECLARATIONS

After locating your suffering and discovering if it's due to a missing narrative, conflicting narratives, a missing action or ineffective actions, you are now in condition to make a declaration.

Declarations are the closest things we have to magic. They are the announcement of a new possibility and new action.

> **Declaration (n): A powerful statement describing a specific outcome, either desired or not desired, and always accompanied by action.**

Why are declarations important and necessary to create the life narrative that you want? When you create declarations that define what is forbidden, required, or allowed, you are painting a picture of what is acceptable and what is not. A powerful declaration states conditions that you will and will not tolerate, closes the possibilities that aren't consistent, and always requires action. Here are three additional things to consider when crafting a declaration.

1. **It needs to be public:** Statements of intention cannot exist in a vacuum. This doesn't mean you have to publish your declarations in the local paper. But it does mean you need to state it out loud, putting yourself on record for having made the declaration. This also puts you in the situation where people choose sides, as to whether they will support or oppose you. This isn't always the most comfortable feeling, but it is necessary to make the declaration something real, versus a passing fancy or fleeting idea of something you may want but don't declare for. It's easy to say, "I'm declaring in favor of world peace." Nobody will oppose that and there is no specific action attached. That's not a declaration; it's just a really good and popular idea. A declaration is not a wish.

2. **It needs to be specific.** When President Kennedy declared that the United States would put a man on the moon and bring him back alive by a certain date, he established what the action was, what the result was, and set a timeline in which it would have to occur to be considered a successful declaration. If you can't measure it, you can't manage it. Generating metrics is the best way to observe actions and manage change. Without clear metrics nothing can be measured and therefore be deemed a success or a failure. Kennedy didn't say "someday." Well "someday" there may be a second coming; that tells me nothing. He set a date, a measurable benchmark. This is crucial because it organizes

action such that an outside observer can tell if the declaration is on its way to being fulfilled or not.

3. **It needs to be supported and realized through actions with measurable results (metrics).** It is impossible for one person to declare World Peace.

DECLARING INDEPENDENCE

One of the most famous documents in history, and one of the two that founded America, begins with a declaration. I'm not referring to the Declaration of Independence, but rather the document that came afterward, the United States Constitution. The remarkable thing about this declaration was how it completely inverted the historical understanding of how power is granted. The colonists had brought with them, across the Atlantic, a tradition of power being granted from the sovereign to the nobles, with only a small amount left over for the people. Before our independence, this is how the English government set up via the Magna Carta under King John in 1215. This was a far more liberal arrangement than existed in most countries of the world at the time. The idea was to avoid rebellion by the nobles. They apparently weren't too concerned about rebellion by the people.

The U.S. Constitution flipped that hierarchy upside down, creating natural, rather than sovereign law, where power is held for and by the people; where power is granted by God rather than by a King. Our constitution is founded on the declaration that the government is the servant of the people, not the master, and the contents reflect that declaration. From the original clauses to the amendments, everything in the Constitution specifies *what is required, what is allowed, and what is forbidden* in the governing of this new nation.

The Bill of Rights, particularly the 9th and 10th amendments, is an example of a government of limited and enumerated powers. What the founders meant is that if it wasn't on the list no one could later claim that the founders merely forgot to put it there. This is also why taxation of income, prohibition of alcohol and universal suffrage required additional Constitutional amendments; they were outside of the original coverage area of what's required, what's allowed, and what is forbidden.

Our founding fathers clearly put a lot of thought, specificity, and intention into the narrative of this new nation they were building. What is written down is more likely to be acted upon, and these men weren't taking any chances with the fate of their experiment. The overall lesson here is that the specificity of your declarations will lead to increased chance of success in the building of a nation or in shifting your life narrative. In America, the grant of power is from the people to the government, not the other way around. This was a new narrative about how power exists, who has it, and who can exercise it. This narrative shift explains a great deal, not only of America's historical prosperity, but also of other nations that follow freedom.

AVOIDING THE KOOL-AID

The people you choose to surround yourself with will certainly have an effect on the declarations you make. Some will get behind you and support your declarations, but others will oppose you. For those brave enough to make a declaration in the first place, be prepared to hear things like: "Well that's just silly. Don't you know that is impossible? I mean how could that ever happen for you? That's a foolish thing for you to say." There's a choosing of sides that occurs. People will either be with you or against you. Because how can someone really be with you, after just saying that they're against the thing you've decided to be true for your life? This is something I want you to be aware of before we continue defining what makes a strong declaration. There's a real chance that you're going to finish this book all pumped up and enthusiastic, like a sprinter out of the blocks, ready to take on the world with your newfound declarations, only to have someone in your life (or more than one person) announce that you're a fool. Ask yourself, if you've made a declaration about what you will or will not tolerate in life, and you are mocked for it, will that be enough to make you stop? Or is your declaration strong enough to keep going no matter what? And it's not just the mortals who will stand in your way either.

There's a saying that the universe will almost always oppose bold declarations; the bolder they are, the more powerful the obstacles thrown in your path. The most important thing you can do is take immediate actions that are consistent with your declarations. For example, for me "I will not be dependent" translated to "go to school and get the skills needed to be independent." Because ultimately, it's not that other person or people who are killing the declaration you've made. They don't have that power. But if their beliefs prevent you from taking action, then you have given them that power. It's not their words that can cause the failure of a declaration, but rather your believing them. You either drink their Kool-Aid or say no thank you and take action as planned.

This is also the big danger about being disabled in America (and I would imagine in most places, but this is my experience). It's not that life is so hard. It's that if you drink the Kool-Aid and believe what *others* think it is to be disabled, life can indeed be extremely difficult. Life is intrinsically difficult no matter who you are. Life doesn't particularly care about me more than it does the other guy. There's a Buddhist saying that the universe is abundant, but indifferent.

I credit my friend Stan Leopard, the son of a protestant minister who then became a practicing Buddhist, for teaching me this. This theory contradicts the notion in Christianity that God cares about the virtuous and will encourage, support, help, defend, protect, and bring prosperity to those who believe, tithe, and are righteous. In Buddhism, the story is that if you take certain actions, you will find the universe to be abundant, but the universe doesn't actually "care" one way or the other what you decide to do. The universe is not your life coach or your mother. It's your choice. There's no master plan for your life that will reward your piety. However, there are abundant opportunities and possibilities if you take the actions. Big change takes big courage. Even to make the declaration and endure any opposition takes courage. None of this is easy, but nothing is as bitter as being stuck with what you have declared to be unacceptable. It is, of course, a matter of personal choice which theory you choose to accept for your own life. In addition to not being a rocket scientist, I am also not a spiritual leader. I do, however, believe that the universe is abundant and indifferent.

DENIAL

It is vital to have strong declarations and never waiver from them. I've often observed that people don't always see it this way. Sometimes, when obstacles occur between a person and his or her goal, it sets off a chain reaction of compromise and rationalization. They tell themselves and others, "Oh well, I didn't want that job anyway," and head off in a different direction. This is a great example of how to end up somewhere different than where you wanted to go; justifications are nothing but course alterations in disguise. They are tranquilizing narratives.

In the moment, however, it is a deceptively minor thing that your mind talks you into believing is the right thing to do. You wanted the job, getting the job went with your narrative, but when you didn't get it, suddenly there was the Kool-Aid to drink so you would believe you never wanted it in the first place. That way, you will not have failed. Justifications can sound good, but they are Kool-Aid. "Those grapes were sour anyway." "I didn't really want the job. I didn't want to be independent. Welfare is easier. A lot of good people are on welfare."

Incidentally, I call this the "socialism for me but not for thee" theory. Remember what Margaret Thatcher said about the subject, "The problem with socialism is that eventually you run out of other people's money."

Nevertheless, with these justifications that the job doesn't matter and welfare will do just fine, the narrative then curves in a different direction. This creates the real risk that months, years, or even decades later you wake up in a life that seems normal. It's the life you've always had and it fits you like an old suit. But just as you're waking, in the twilight zone between then and now, you suddenly remember your original declaration for the original narrative that you wanted, really wanted. There's nothing specifically wrong with your life. The old suit is well worn and fits just fine, no holes, tears, or missing buttons. But when what you once wanted flashes through your mind, it brings with it the question: "How did my narrative bring me to this point and why am I suddenly finding it unacceptable? How did this happen?" The short answer is, that at one point, in one moment, you made yourself believe that you didn't want something that you actually did want. You lied to yourself. You deleted a declaration and the course of your life changed. You went backwards into drift.

There is a quote in the book/movie *No Country for Old Men*: "If the rule you followed brought you to this, of what use was the rule?" Or in other words, if all the steps you took in life brought you to this moment, what makes you think those were the right steps? Realistically speaking, there is a multitude of moments in your life when a decision you make can shift your narrative. The moments might not even be the Earth shattering ones either; they could be small, subtle, and quiet as a church mouse. If you consistently make choices based on your declarations, of what you will and will not tolerate in life, you will remain in control of your narrative. But if you decide to dismiss or justify changing a declaration, it can have drastic consequences.

PRESIDENTS

It was two years before the fall of the Soviet Union and I was about to meet the then president of the oval office, George H.W. Bush.

This wasn't the first president I'd shaken hands with. Back in the early 80s, Uncle Jake arranged a meeting with President Reagan. The Bush meeting, however, was based on my own merit. Senator Bob Dole had just appointed me to the United States Commission on Civil Rights. There was a ceremony in the Rose Garden where I was announced to the press, and then my guide dog and I were escorted by Secret Service into the Oval Office.

I found President Bush to be much more impressive in person than on TV. He was much taller than I thought.

Now, you may be wondering how a blind person would know how tall someone is; or anything else about him or her. Over the years, I've developed a new ability for being an observer. This isn't based on eyesight or even hearing. Those are just physical senses. One's capacity for being an observer, almost like a new dimension, is based on distinctions like what they can "listen" for rather than simply hear. I can tell a lot about a person's size, age, weight, and mood in a short conversation, while also making pretty accurate assessments about them as a person like personality, character, etc.

When I was introduced to President Bush, the first thing he did was kneel to shake my dog's paw. The White House photographer captured the moment.

Mother saw the photo, got very excited and exclaimed in a moment of maternal hyperbole, "Russell I always *knew* that presidents would kneel down to you!"

CHAPTER 11
ACTIONS

The rooster thinks that his crowing causes the sun to rise. The Native Americans think that rain dances cause rain to happen. Actions without understanding hold little weight.

—Russell Redenbaugh

Landing Metal Birds

D uring World War II some South Pacific islands were used as staging areas for American military inventory. Hulking silver metal cargo planes would routinely land and soldiers would rush out and unload all types of cargo in giant boxes; food, batteries, weapons, survival gear, housing, equipment, and more. Then the plane would take off to refill with more cargo and the process repeated this way throughout the war. Well as it turns out, those cargo planes and soldiers were being watched, and carefully.

The South Pacific island natives peered down at the runways from hilltops, ducking behind bushes, and hiding behind trees, fascinated by the big metal birds. Where did these birds come from, they wondered, and why were they always full of food and survival supplies? The islanders, of course, had no understanding of what an airplane was, so they decided that the big metal birds came from the heavens. Further, they made note of the exact procedures required to call forth the birds from the heavens. They memorized the sequence of events that needed to happen to bless the people on the ground with food and supplies. The islanders thought they were witnessing a true miracle, and they began to worship the big metal birds. Conferring with the tribal elders, they decided that every native and his family should learn all the steps necessary to please the gods that sent these planes and the precious life-giving cargo inside. Anthropologists would later name this a religion, the Cargo Cult.

In the meantime, the islanders benefited tremendously from the existence of those Army Air Corps bases during WWII. The military created jobs for the natives, resulting in much better food and conditions on the islands. They no longer had to survive only on fish, coconuts, yams, and whatever else they could grow. Their conditions improved drastically from their former lives as hunters, gatherers, farmers, and fishermen.

When the war ended and the military cleared out, they left quite a bit of cargo behind, including the air traffic control tower and runway where the giant metal birds once landed. The islanders were not worried. They had studied for years all the physical actions needed to make the metal birds and their cargo arrive from the heavens. So they sat in the tower, in their tribal clothes, wearing aviation headsets and saying things into the microphones. They chanted prayers to the gods to make the metal birds come back. Some of them ran up and down the runway, waving their arms the way the soldiers had as they were landing the planes. Still others stood off to the side of the runway, peering into the sky, waiting to unload the cargo once the birds landed. The birds never came. So the islanders blamed themselves and vowed to the gods that they would try harder. This was their only explanation for why the metal birds were not coming—they must not be working hard enough. But of course, the birds never came. This was the scene that anthropologists found when they stumbled upon these "cargo cult cultures" years after World War II had ended.

The islanders' declaration was: we will call forth the metal birds and all their cargo to supply our island. However, since they were not working from the right "understanding" of what was actually happening, the narrative they created simply mimicked the military's narrative. The natives then mimicked the soldiers' actions to bring that narrative to life. When it didn't work, they continued to mimic, but with more intensity, working around the clock in shifts, desperately trying to please the gods so they would send down the metal birds.

This may sound unbelievable or even comical to you and of course we're talking about a very primitive people with a limited understanding of the world. But if you think about it, aren't there people out there in our present day civilized society, who try the same thing? They admire someone else's success and decide that simply mimicking the successful person's actions will bring them the same success.

"If I do every single thing that Tony Robbins has done in his life to be successful, make the same decisions he has, the same stock investments, dress the way he dresses, and act the way he acts, I will be as successful as he," they think.

They mimic without a full understanding of everything that Tony actually did to become a success. Then, after a period of time they wonder why they don't have Tony Robbins' success. This is not rewriting or shifting your narrative. It is imitating someone else's with the hopes of achieving the same results. Mimicking without full understanding will never produce the same results. This reminds me of some of the "tips and tricks" thinking that is so prevalent. "Do these ten things and your life will change." As far as I know that only worked once, and it involved Moses with a stone tablet on a mountaintop.

Tips, steps, and other paint-by-number ways of thinking really do a disservice in that they hide the complex way in which the world really works. There is no easy way to change, but there is a simple and profound way. There are no "10 easy steps" to change the world or even your world.

My friend and student, Leslie, learned this while attending one of my investment seminars at Miraval Spa. She said that I taught her how to "see," and found the irony of learning to see from a blind person absolutely delicious.

Leslie Bruhn, a successful CPA on the California central coast, recounted to me as we talked about this book, "I remember the world opening up for me as you spoke. But then I looked around the room and saw to my surprise, that nobody else seemed to be experiencing the same lightning bolts. At first I thought maybe I was reading too much into your lessons and maybe I was crazy. And it hit me! They weren't having the same experience that I was because they had come to the seminar looking for quick tips and simple formulas that they could take home and use to get rich overnight. They didn't get that you were teaching them how to see—how to observe—and then shift their entire money narrative as a result."

Mimicking may appear to work to a certain degree in some things. Investing, if you read all the tips and tricks, do what others do, and follow directions the very best you can do is get average returns that may only appear sufficient. Again, you don't know what you don't know. But if you want to be really excellent, and get the best results, you must gain a much deeper understanding of what is really occurring and then innovate from inside that place. Full understanding may take a lifetime, but the only test of knowing is doing.

EFFECTIVE ACTION

You've located a limiting narrative, and taken the most important action of making a bold declaration. But the job of shifting your narrative is not complete. You must continue to take effective actions that move you toward fulfilling your declaration by moving away from what you will not tolerate and toward that which you have announced you will have.

Action and motion are not the same. The cargo cult natives were doing motions, but they were not taking effective action. In the same way, action and motivation are not the same.

Motivation only lasts if it is coupled with a new set of actions. Shifting your narrative is not about being motivated for a moment, but rather about taking action permanently through new habits and behaviors.

Also, action and activity are not the same. For example, imagine you are at Deer Valley Ski Resort and see someone skiing in the distance. The activity they are doing is clearly skiing. But what is their real action? Action requires an interpretation of the circumstances and setting. The skier may be working on ski patrol, recreating on vacation, or training for the winter Olympics.

Louisa Gilder is the daughter of George Gilder, a highly influential thinker on technology, information theory and economics and also a longtime friend and mentor. George has written nineteen books, several of which have been worldwide bestsellers. Several years back, Louisa made the declaration that she was going to write a book she'd been contemplating on quantum physics. She wanted to write the book, had all the knowledge and information at her disposal to do the job, and knew that this was the perfect time to get it done. However, Louisa suddenly stalled a bit because she didn't have the ideal setting to take more effective actions. She realized that her family home was too active a place for a first-time writer. So her father George encouraged Louisa to come out to California to stay with Natalia and me. George is a spectacularly good writer and Louisa was a very smart, confident young woman who didn't have any self-limiting narratives like "I'm not good enough," "I can't do this," or "I'm just a girl," holding her back. Far from it, she graduated Dartmouth with a 4.0 GPA and was on Dartmouth's ski team giving her the discipline of an elite athlete. She just needed support in the actions piece, and we were happy to help.

Fortunately, Louisa was bright enough. She knew she needed support and structure and gladly drove out west. Sure enough, once she was staying in our guest bedroom, Louisa got the focus she needed to take action and complete her book. Much of that, ended up being our constant encouragements, "Go down to your room. Don't come back up until you've written 1,000 words."

Louisa finished *The Age of Entanglement: When Quantum Physics was Reborn,* and it was very well received. She is currently working on her second book (not in our guest room this time).

The lesson about action from Louisa's story is that after making a declaration you need to take a number of other actions to achieve it. For Louisa, she needed to literally remove herself from the distractions of family, friends, and college. Fortunately, her father George was the writing coach and we merely provided the location and "structure" for her to take the effective actions needed to complete her declaration of writing a book on quantum physics.

The reason that action is by far the most challenging piece of the Shift model is that it's the nature of human beings to procrastinate. It is also easy for us to remain asleep in the "drift." Again, by drift we mean unconscious to our procrastination. For example, many tell themselves,

"I'll start saving for retirement next year" until it's finally too late. We can create the most specific, determined declarations in the world, and then shape them with powerful narratives, but without effective action, it's all talk and pipe dreams. In publishing, this is why deadlines exist and editors to enforce those deadlines, essentially telling writers "go down to your room and don't come back until you've written your 1,000 words." It's also why we have managers, bosses, and for some, coaches, mentors, and consultants to both hold us accountable for completion and help keep us on course. In my experience being held accountable to action and getting guidance from an outside party, creates the best results.

THE DISCIPLINE TO NOT DO WHAT YOU WANT

There's nothing more useless than a runway that's behind you or altitude that's above you.
—Russell Redenbaugh

Successful people are excellent at closing possibilities. That's the nature of choice—when you choose one, it eliminates others. I have a friend named Rusty Holden. I first met him on an airplane and concluded on the spot that he was completely crazy—but in a good way. He is a real life mad scientist who had developed many different inventions in nuclear power and nuclear isotopes, but had commercialized none of them. Rusty didn't have a problem with ideas; he had a problem with completion. He didn't want to give up on anything that might become something. And when you have that many potential "somethings" how can you tell which is the winning idea?

I knew that if he didn't pick one idea and commercialize it, he could remain a really smart, but poor, mad scientist. I started to help Rusty close other attractive possibilities in order to pursue just one by asking a series of simple but leading questions.

"Are you married Rusty?"

"Well, yes."

"Happily?" I asked.

"Yes," he answered.

"Well, when you got married, you closed other possibilities, didn't you? Are you sorry you did that?" I asked.

"Well, no," he said.

"Good," I said, "Now which one of these good ideas will you marry?"

Next, I flipped the conversation into one of scientific reasoning. Sometimes the best-received advice is spoken in the recipient's language.

"Start with the end in mind," I told Rusty.

"What do you mean by that?" he said.

"Which invention is most likely to produce a short-term liquidity event?" I asked, referring to the end goal of commercializing the invention and creating a profitable company.

"Hmmm…" he said. "Medical, because nuclear power plants are impossible to build in the U.S."

"Good. So let's take all the nuclear power plan projects off the table. Now, which of your medical inventions is most likely to find a market wherein somebody would buy your company, or more importantly, invest in it once you do proof of concept?"

As a result, Rusty picked one invention to commercialize. By finding a way to eliminate all possibilities except one, the mad scientist was able to move out of overwhelm and into effective action.

From Rusty, I was reminded that brilliance is not enough. What the universe rewards is the person who sticks with a single idea and pursues it relentlessly. It's not just about being smart. If it were, the world would be crawling with many more legendary success stories in every discipline. As I told Rusty, "Focus, focus, focus. Do one thing, do one thing again, and then do it more." As tempting as it is to want to do everything, the discipline to avoid that temptation is the difference between finishing something successfully and quitting in overwhelm.

The state of overwhelm is really the inability to close possibilities. This results in a bad mood, and inaction, which some people call procrastination. Bad moods show up when you're not in purposeful action. It all starts with closing possibilities. Similar to how there is a very low return on investment being the "victim," there is also an extremely low ROI on being unwilling to choose one possibility and act. Both, by the way, are declarations. You are either making the declaration that you will make a choice or making the declaration that you will not choose. Not choosing is a choice.

In addition to procrastination, it is also in our human nature to say, "yes" repeatedly until we are finally completely overcommitted.

For instance, we have a bad habit of asking our staff to do more than they can realistically get done. This is definitely our weakness, but in our defense, we do let new employees know this when we hire them. We tell them, "Now we will ask, and ask, and ask, but it's up to you to have the skill to say, 'Well sure Russell, I'll do that, but that means I won't be able to do this other thing.'" We let new employees know that if they can't learn this, they won't be very successful working for us. The good ones learn how to say, "No." The bad ones wander off.

Now this may seem cruel, but if you think about it, you are faced with this situation every day. The only difference is, you're not being told about it outright. Your boss, the PTA at your child's school, and your friends are not collectively saying, "Now, we're going to try and pile so many requests and responsibilities on you that if you don't say no to some of them, you will crack." It's your job to say no. If you can't successfully say no, overwhelm happens.

TIME TO ACT

Taking effective action isn't easy, but that's not because it is intrinsically difficult. Instead, most of us simply don't know how to do it. Here are some of the distinctions and steps I have successfully used to change my life.

Promises

Promises are the way we interact successfully with others. Would you rely on someone, a friend, or a business, which repeatedly failed to keep their promises? Clearly not. In America, we live in a deep cultural confusion about what is a promise. Some of us honestly believe we have not made a promise if we don't say the words, "I promise." This breakdown causes mistrust and suspicion. A powerful way to separate yourself from the uncoordinated masses and become effective is to implement two "promise strategies." 1) Listen for promises in all conversations. 2) Be aware of making promises in all conversations.

A promise exists when four conditions are present. The first two are that there is a listener and speaker who each understands what a promise is. For example, a toddler cannot understand, nor make a promise. A sixteen-year-old may understand what a promise is, but we should seriously doubt their capacity to carry out multi-year promises.

The third element of a promise is Conditions of Satisfaction. This is "what" the promisor has agreed to provide, and the more understandable by each party the better. For example, around the house a man may promise his wife to do all the shopping for the family's July 4th picnic. She accepts, and when he arrives home with three-dozen hot dogs, buns, chips, and two cases of beer, the husband is mystified by the wife's unhappiness. Clearly there was no meeting of the minds about what a shopping list for the picnic meant. An effective communication would have been more specific about what is on and not on the shopping list.

The husband did go shopping for the party. But his promise to do the shopping for the picnic was not fulfilled.

Another example occurs frequently in business, specifically meetings. A CEO calls his top executives to an important "strategy session." The CFO, COO, head of sales, and director of marketing prepare extensively, each producing deep examinations into their silos. But when they arrive the CEO reads his agenda to discuss high-level, outside-of-the-box ideas about the company's strategy in ten years. Since each team member assumed that "strategy session" meant a review of his or her respective roles, no one is prepared and all that is discussed is scheduling the next meeting. An effective communication from the CEO would have specified the condition of satisfaction for a "strategy brainstorming" meeting.

The fourth element of a promise is time, or by when. We all know about the immovability of deadlines from many parts of life: taxes due, school paper due, license renewal due. Time is often clear and imposed by outside forces. But the time that destroys effective action is time that is not imposed by an outsider like the DMV or IRS. It's the time we self-impose like, "I'll do it later or at end of next week." To be a rigorous promise, time must be either specified or clearly understood. For example, a manager who promises to "deliver the report by the end of the week" is setting himself up for an unsatisfied boss. Although in America this would not get him fired, it doesn't increase his value in the least. A more valuable manager makes a promise that, "The report will be on your desk by 4 p.m. Thursday, does that work for you?"

For my partner at Kairos Capital Advisors, James Juliano, the learning began before he even started on the job. On the day in my office that I made him an employment offer, he and I made a deal, which means to me we both made a promise, that he would accept or reject my offer by a certain date. As a fresh university graduate and busy

Wall Street rookie, James did not have the same refined understanding about promises as I did. After alerting his investment-banking employer about his notice to leave and take a new job, James accepted my offer. However, he accepted 8 hours past the "promised" deadline.

My response was, "I am happy to hear your decision, but my offer is withdrawn."

Now, with no job, he had learned the importance of promises. Chastened, James offered to come work for free as an "economic research volunteer" until he'd proven his value. We let him do that, but only let him suffer without pay a short time. To this day that man, now my business partner, friend, and a most trusted advisor, has never lost sight of the importance of promises. The word promise was never said, of course, but clearly with the job offer, promises were being exchanged.

At bottom, a promise is a commitment between two people who understand what a promise is. Promises are powerful and allow us to coordinate our actions with others. They make the world work. When you listen and speak more rigorously regarding promises, you're ready for the next step.

Requests and Offers

We are request machines. We live our lives making requests, unfortunately most are sloppy. For example, in long-term relationships it's common to say, "I'm tired," or "I'm hungry," or "I'm bored." However, in the context of the relationship, these are requests masquerading as announcements. The way to make a more rigorous request is to apply the conditions of a promise. Make sure both parties understand it is a request, with sufficient conditions of satisfaction and a time certain for completion.

An offer is a conditional promise. Like a request, a rigorous offer must meet the requirement of a promise like conditions of satisfaction and time of completion. For example, "I offer to paint your kitchen for

$500 next Tuesday." Offers are far more powerful than requests because they create value if your offer delivers on something the receiver wants.

Let's pull these distinctions together into an example of effective actions. A wife and mother of two makes a declaration to her family, "I will become competent enough playing the cello to play in our community orchestra in less than one year." She follows up on that declaration by taking the following actions.

She makes promises, like to her husband. "I won't spend more than five hours per week learning to play the cello, and I will organize my lessons and practice times so that they do not interfere with after school homework and family meal times."

She makes requests, like finding a local cello instructor and requesting to be a student. She makes sure to clarify what will be taught, what times it will be taught, and what payment will be made.

She makes offers, like volunteering to help the cello instructor with his billing/accounting/business paperwork in exchange for sitting in on lessons with other students.

Through effective actions like these, she is on her way to fulfilling her declaration.

DESIGNING FOR ACTION

Here are some useful rules that will help keep your declarations and supporting actions coherent to increase your chances of affecting change.

Mentorship

Mentorship is a powerful tool in shifting narratives, because mentors have the advantage of seeing the big picture, including different perspectives on a topic or situation that the mentee is blind to.

Case in point, one of our employees who helped us with tasks around the house was working on her MBA and told me how overwhelmed she was by the complexities of the financial lessons, particularly accounting. I decided to spend some time with her to help change her narrative.

"You know," I told her one day over lunch, "finance is not intrinsically complicated. Complicated is an assessment that's made by the observer who doesn't have enough distinctions to see the simplicity of whatever it is they're learning."

In other words, something becomes complicated when you look at it from the point of view that doesn't see the basic fundamentals of what is happening. By having a narrative that learning accounting was hard, she had created a climate of stress and resistance around her learning. So I helped shift this by showing her different perspectives of her "finance is hard" narrative; ones that she hadn't previously seen.

The student can only look from where they look. You can't realistically tell someone to "look from a different perspective" because they don't really know what that means. "See it differently" is not an operational instruction. Instead, and as I did with this young woman, the mentor's message should be: "There are people who understand this phenomenon. From where you are as a beginner, you simply cannot see the big picture that I see." And from there, you take them step-by-step into the picture, widening the lens with each basic principle and lesson.

Soon into the conversation, I could feel the wall of "this is too hard to learn" resistance beginning to crumble as she saw that learning accounting was no different than a more complicated checkbook.

Mentoring is never a one-way street. For me, the best way to learn something is to teach it to someone who has no idea what you're talking about. If you can understand a topic well enough to explain it to a beginner, then you have truly mastered the subject. This means being able to take the complexity out and boil down to the essence. A good teacher or mentor can help the student learn a topic in a profoundly simple way. Teachers who confuse their students by making complex things even more complex, might not understand their subjects as deeply as they think. The only reason that I am at all "qualified" to take on the role of mentor in this book, is because I've been studying what it takes to shift narratives for most of my life. It is because I lived within the Shift model that I am able to make it accessible for you and others.

I met Bill Coleman in 2000 in Salt Lake City while I was looking into buying a bankrupted 3,500-acre ranch. The plan was to convert it into five to twenty-acre residential horse properties. Bill connected me with the people I needed to know to make the project happen and in return (as I have the habit of doing) I shared my Shift model. One of our first conversations took place as we drove down a long two-lane highway to look at the ranch property.

"What do you care about in life?" I asked him at one point.

Bill rambled on about family, feel good things, work, the housing industry, current events, and other things obviously central to his world.

"Well you know that each of the things you listed is something you care about, but how passionate are you really about any of the things you just listed? How rich and meaningful are they to you, especially in regards to where you want your life to go?"

He soon realized that none of his present declarations prompted strong enough answers. From there, he built a narrative based on discovering how he could have a greater impact on his world. In other words, he asked the right questions to find out what others cared about, and then performed the actions to deliver it to them. This has, in turn, added a new level of depth and intensity to Bill's world.

"What I've done is pay it forward too; the Shift model," Bill told me recently while we were fly fishing in Park City, Utah. "Finding out so much about my own narrative has changed my life, and it's been exciting to pass it on."

The impromptu role of mentor that I took on with Bill is not unusual for me. Perhaps because of the things I've gone through, perhaps because I'm a teacher by nature, or a combination of the two, this tends to happen for many people I encounter. Reading between the lines, hearing the things they're not saying, I identify a way to help them change their declarations, create new actions, and shift their narrative. As a mentor for life I can't help myself; there's no off switch.

The challenge is finding enough good mentees to receive this knowledge. Yes that's right, there is a shortage of good mentees for mentors who wish to guide them. Mentors don't suffer fools gladly. Therefore, if you are good mentee, you can always find the best mentors. You are the scarce resource, not them.

So, what makes a good mentee? Surrender. A good mentee is able to suspend suspicion, mistrust, and hostility, and receive the information. This doesn't mean that they turn their brains off and drink the Kool-Aid. But it does mean the temporary suspension of disbelief. They replace "Well that can't be right!" with more of a curiosity, "That's so different from what I've been taught. Tell me why you say that." Curiosity versus cynicism. A good mentee is also fascinated by a deep understanding of the topic at hand (whether life, their vocation, business, etc.) versus simply collecting "tips and techniques" to tide them over.

There is a similar distinction between mentors and teachers. While teaching is often about the transfer of information, mentoring is about the transfer of skilled capacity into action. Knowing is only proven by doing, and a mentor builds that capacity for action within the mentee.

A good mentor also holds a vision for the mentee, of what he or she can become, especially when they can't see the forest for the trees and become tangled up in challenges and discouragement. The mentor continues to support them along in the narrative, managing their mood, and reinforcing that knowledge is only useful when attached to a capacity for action. A mentor supports the narrative of a possible future (assuming the mentee does his or her part to follow the lessons and take the correct actions).

Relative progress must be measured. This does not mean comparing the mentee's progress against the mentor's much more significant life experience.

The lesson here for mentors is not to produce a negative assessment of the mentee based on a very unfair mentor/mentee comparison. For mentees it is to avoid standing against a yardstick so tall that they can never possibly measure up.

Dr. Fernando Flores is a philosopher, Silicon Valley entrepreneur, and Chilean politician that I met during the 1980s in Silicon Valley. Seeing the value of his knowledge and experience, I attached myself to him, and ran one of his companies. I always felt that more so than the paychecks he wrote for me, the most value I received from Dr. Flores was in his knowledge.

A successful mentoring relationship is mutually beneficial. Each party, mentor and mentee, have to be satisfied that they are receiving value; the scales have to balance.

Now some people I've seen have a somewhat distorted view of what a mentor "should" offer them. They see a mentor as an unlimited Rolodex of contacts, connections, and opportunities. This is by no means mutually beneficial—a mentor connecting a mentee with his network in exchange for what? In addition, the mentor is taking on an enormous risk, putting his reputation on the line. Imagine if he hooks the mentee up with his network, which took him years, possibly decades to build trust and rapport with, and the mentee fails or behaves badly. It would be very difficult for the mentor to rebuild that trust and rapport with his network. Relationships are infinitely more valuable than money. You can always make your money back, but not your reputation.

Overall, mentoring is a much more intimate and more trust-based relationship than any sort of coaching or guidance. Throughout the book, you've met some of the people whom I've mentored along the way. They are all recipients of the Shift message that I came up with years ago, most of them willing recipients I'd like to believe. You've also met some of my mentors, like Art Laffer, George Gilder, and Dr. Flores.

As I've moved through these relationships and others, I've learned that a mentor must be willing—and even eager—to see his or her mentee outgrow them. A true mentor celebrates this, rather than letting ego get in the way and feeling discarded or useless. I say this because all too many times I've seen "not so good" mentors form an emotionally needy narrative with their mentee, stifling them from growing too far and expanding beyond the mentor. Some parents do this as well, which is unfortunate since the job of a good parent is to be put out of a job.

Mini Max

Phil Migliarese, who owns Balance Studios in Philadelphia with his brother Ricardo, is a 5th degree Brazilian jiu-jitsu black belt with an impressive track record as both competitor and trainer.

We had just finished a lesson one day when Phil shared how he was thinking about opening his first gym.

"Well, couldn't that be financially risky?" I asked him.

"Yes," he said, "but there really isn't any other way to do it, is there?"

I told him, "Actually there are two strategies you can pursue and both relate to the fighting strategies I've seen you use in tournaments. You've never used the maxi-max strategy, meaning maximize your maximum return. You never do the flashy thing that could work spectacularly, but if you don't do it perfectly you could lose it all."

"That's true," Phil agreed.

"You do mini-max instead, meaning minimize your maximum regret. In fighting your maximum regret is a loss, not a win that is less flashy. So, your fight strategy is the tortoise rather than the hare. You win by little increments. You let the other person have your way. So, what are the ways you do this in opening a business? How could you still start your own gym while minimizing your maximum loss?"

Bingo. Light bulb on! Phil got what I was saying when I connected a new business challenge with something extremely familiar to him, his fighting style. Phil now calls what I taught him "business jiu-jitsu." The two-minute video below features the two of us demonstrating some moves on the mat.

https://www.youtube.com/watch?v=3xty8T2L7VM

Mini-max strategies you likely already use include carrying life, health, car, and excess liability insurance. You prepare for a bad outcome and hope it doesn't happen. Now that you see this as minimizing your maximum regret, review your coverage to make sure they are high enough.

Mini-max is one of the strategies I use rigorously for designing everything I do. Most people go through life over optimistically, with hopes and expectations that are not solidly based in evidence. Minimizing your maximum regret recognizes that not all plans stay on the "happy path" and bad things do happen. When most people design an action they think, "I want this, so I'll do X." Instead, a mini-max strategy starts with the possibility of a breakdown or failure, and designs the action to mitigate that potential damage.

STRUCTURE OF INCENTIVES

An incentive is a payment or benefit that may cause a change in behavior in order to collect. Children learn about incentives early. Eat your peas and you'll get dessert. Remember the job jar with chores and prices of completion written on pieces of paper? From this initial beginning, incentives become an increasing part of our "structures" as we mature.

The structure of incentives shapes our behaviors. We all tend to do that which is consistent with the incentives, as we understand them. Some incentives are so clear and powerful that the action is easy. The consequence of not paying the IRS is going to jail, and most of us are sufficiently incented to pay without protest.

Beyond this obvious example, the structure of incentives is too often confused or lost when we design our actions. In not understanding their importance, you design actions ignorant of the forces that influence your and others' behaviors.

Residential real estate sales commission is typically six percent of the sales price. You may naively think your incentives and the selling agent's are aligned, higher the selling price, higher the agent's commission. But wait, this is wrong, as proven by Steven Levitt in his 2005 bestseller *Freakonomics: A Rogue Economist Explores the Hidden Side of Everything*. The real deal is the agent maximizes income from a quick sale, and a quick sale is most often produced from a lower price. To secure a higher price requires longer time on market and additional marketing expense paid by the agent. To test his hypothesis, Levitt compared the length of time that agent-owned houses were on the market versus their clients' homes. Agents behaved differently when selling their own homes than when selling your home, because the structure of incentives is different.

What is the structure of incentives for elite universities' admissions committees? The title "admission committee" leads you to believe their job is to admit the best students. It is not. From the viewpoint of the student, the admissions committee's job is not to admit you. It is to find reasons why your application belongs in the discard pile. Those reasons to not admit line up with each schools structure of incentives. Do they want a well-balanced student body or a higher than average number of "eccentrics"? Knowing the committees' structure of incentives influences where and how a student applies.

What is the structure of incentives for traditional financial advisors? The nice man helping you select the correct mutual fund for your retirement will receive compensation based on the products he sells you. There is a conflict of interest when he sells you an investment product to earn commission while telling you that product is in your best interest. It may be, but the structure of incentives forces commission-based advisors to frequently make poor choices for the client.

Always stop and ask the question "Who benefits?" as the German philosopher Hegel taught. James and I use this all the time in our investment advisory businesses when making political and economic assessments. Another way we say it is, "Follow the money." People will generally move from their self-interest and rarely from yours. We invest our own and our clients' money following our narrative of "Policy Based Investing" because government economic policies set the rules of the game, and later the structure of incentives, for companies, sectors, and entire countries. When government policies change, the structure of incentives change, and we work diligently to identify when and where those changes happen.

Think about our recent experience with technology rapidly changing the entire structure of incentives. As George Gilder wrote in *Microcosm* in 1989, "The transformation from moving atoms to bits at light speed will topple the structures of power." We have seen the elimination of entire industries based on technology changing the structure of incentives. The music and book industries are two of the best examples. No one sent a "memo" that brick-and-mortar music and bookstores would so rapidly disappear, but the structure of incentives caused their customers to flee.

Following the structure of incentives works at the country level as well, how could it not? French president Hollande decided to increase taxes on France's wealthiest residences in 2012. Since France, like most countries, taxes on residency, not citizenship, the tax rate hike shifted an important piece of the structure of incentives. When tax rates skyrocketed, wealthy French residents interpreted the law as a request to move to Belgium, where they also speak French.

The above examples demonstrate that the structure of incentives is powerful, present, and subject to rapid change without notice. Well-designed actions must acknowledge this.

We humans are amazing creatures; we can do nearly anything we want. As my dad always said in an early economics lesson, "You can have anything you can pay for."

Working from that starting point, my life has been filled with many victories, many failures, some great accomplishments, and some disappointments. But I did what I have done, have had a great life and it is not over yet. The best may be yet to come. Who really knows? I've already done much more than I ever thought possible since those fifty plus years ago on the day that a homemade rocket explosion changed my life forever.

But despite all that I have accomplished, I often think that I could have done so much more. For instance, I should have written this book sooner.

When I set out to write this book, I thought it would be much more difficult than it turned out to be. I also think that I've produced a better volume than I anticipated when I began. This is not a reflection on the value of my story or the Shift model. This reluctance on my part was purely about the question I kept asking myself whenever the subject of writing a book came up: Who cares?

For years, I found the idea of writing a book about myself a bit self-indulgent and narcissistic. I had the same objection when I was first approached to do the Tedx Talk about my life and even after the talk as I left the stage, I still didn't fully understand what the point was of telling my story. I never wanted to write "just" a biography, to tell my story with no meat built around it. That seemed pointless. If I was going to write a book, it had to be something that offered tools people could use in their lives. This was never to highlight the idea, "oh wow, I'm so special." The point was always to highlight that everyone can be special with the right narrative. The goal was to turn my life story and what I've picked up along the way into an actionable model that people can follow to shift their narrative and live a better life. That was the difference between speaking on stage and writing this book. Once I finally came to this realization, of the difference between telling a story and offering an actionable model for true shift, the whole process began. Perhaps I should have written this book sooner. But at least I finally made it past, "Who cares?"

CLOSING THOUGHTS

We all live in narratives. We have ideas about who we are, what happens to us, and why our situation is as it is. We form stories about the careers we choose, the friends we have and the places we go. These self-generated stories both expand and limit our opportunities. Most of us believe our circumstances produce our narratives. But what if our narratives produce our circumstances?

Whether you believe it or not, you already possess the capability to have more of what you care about. Your narratives are blinding you. A different narrative produces a different you. It's not easy nor is it an instantaneous change. But it can be done. There are tools you can use now to start having more of what you care about. You can't win a gold medal in jiu-jitsu tomorrow, but you can begin shifting your narrative to make that a possibility today.

EPILOGUE
BACK ON THE MAT

September 2015

N ow finish him!" my coach bellowed, screaming above the crowd noise.

Grappling with my opponent, Alexandre "Xande" Ribeiro a 210-pound, seven-time world champion black belt, all I can think is, "Am I *really* doing this at seventy years-old?"

It's the International BJJ Master Senior Jiu-Jitsu Tournament and it's held once a year. It used to be held in Rio de Janeiro, the same place where I experienced my initial victories. Now, it's in Las Vegas where it draws a dramatically larger attendance; tickets were sold out weeks before the registration deadline. There are also more contestants,

3,000 this year and far more than the organizers planned over a two-day period. They ran fourteen simultaneous matches.

But I would not be a contestant in this event. I stopped entering tournaments in 2005 after winning my third world championship. I figured I'd quit while I was ahead and now I'm a decade beyond the upper age limit. They did ask me back to perform a few different demonstrations though. This was my way of thanking the BJJ organization and the sport of jiu-jitsu for all it had done to improve my life.

I flew to Las Vegas with Natalia and my trainer Eduardo days before the event to get ready. I hadn't trained in nearly five weeks, and did I mention I'm now seventy years old? Not that age matters; that's a narrative I discarded long ago when I got into jiu-jitsu at age fifty. For example, and as Natalia reminds me, at the gym I routinely tap out black belts who are in their thirties. But, as I remind her back, "Yes dear, but they aren't world champs, I am. They're young and strong, but I know a different set of moves." The other guys at my gym have caught on, but every once in a while I can catch a new guy. During my training in Las Vegas before the demonstration, I tapped out three black belts. None of these three had seen any of these submissions before now.

"What was THAT?" an opponent exclaimed during one of our practice sessions.

"That was a foot lock," I replied calmly.

"Yeah, but you didn't use your hands!!"

"Yes, it's a foot lock done with my feet," I answered him.

"Yes, but your foot locked my foot," he persisted.

"That's why it's a foot lock," I said.

It's not an age narrative. It's an experience narrative.

Before my match with the 210-pound, seven-time champion, they announced that this would be my last fight, that I was retiring from competition but still continuing to train twice a week. I received a nice ovation from the crowd who clearly, looking at my monster-sized opponent, figured out that it was a demonstration and not a real match. Barring any serious mistakes by Goliath, there's no way I could have defeated him in an open competition.

First he toyed with me, letting me demonstrate some moves for the crowd, like escapes from his guard and takedowns. It was a five-minute match so that took up about four minutes.

With one minute to go, Eduardo yelled to finish him. That was the clue for him not to defend quite so hard and for me to attack. I turned on all the energy I'd been saving and put what's called a knee in the belly. Then I went for a choke, which was pointless since I couldn't come close to getting my good hand around his monster neck and he had his chin down. The only reason I even attempted was to set up an arm lock, to put his attention on defending his neck so his arm was left open. I arm-locked him and he quickly submitted.

Even though it was a pre-planned demonstration, it didn't in any way feel like a simulation to me. When I thumped Goliath back down on the ground—and hard—my heart was pounding with excitement! For me it felt very real.

Nevertheless, afterward Natalia said, "Oh, this is not a real fight?"

"No sweetie, I don't do real fights with big young guys. Well, unless they're new guys who don't know my moves."

Morgan James
Speakers Group

We connect Morgan James published
authors with live and online events
and audiences whom will benefit
from their expertise.